BE A MENSCH

A Legacy of the Holocaust

BE A MENSCH

A Legacy of the Holocaust

By
Alexander Bialywlos White

DEDICATION

I dedicate this book to the memory of my family, so brutally murdered by the Nazis, and to the millions of defenseless, innocent victims of those Nazi beasts.

I also dedicate it to the many heroes who gave their lives to save us survivors from that evil regime.

Credits:
Editing, cover design and typesetting by Dennis and Carol DeFrain,
Goodyear, Arizona

Printed in the United States of America

ACKNOWLEDGEMENTS

Thanks to my wife, Inez, for her patience with my cluttered desk and the many hours on the computer. Thanks also to our son Les for his encouragement or rather insistence that I disclose my tragic experiences. He recorded them years ago at a time when many survivors kept quiet. I did not realize how significant my memories would be for those who have virtually had no extended family because of the Holocaust. I mistakenly kept quiet because I did not want to burden my children with my suffering.

I also recognize the untiring love and devotion from my two daughters Denise and Julie whom I cherish and whose deep love provides me comfort and assists me in my perseverance and the healing of my incurred wounds.

I wish to give special thanks to Dennis DeFrain, Ed.D. (Retired U.S. Army Lt. Col.), for assisting in the preparation of the reprinting of this book and for assisting me in the writing and publication of the book: *Surviving the Holocaust in Siberia – The Diary of Pearl Minz.*

TABLE OF CONTENTS

INTRODUCTION

The word *Mensch* in German means "a human being." In Yiddish the language of the Jews of Eastern Europe with German and Slavic roots, the word *Mensch* denotes something a little more. It means "a special, ideal human being; a person endowed with the finest attributes by Our Creator including charity, kindness, tolerance, honesty and love of mankind." It is up to each individual to develop his or her *Menschlichkeit* to the fullest.

"Be a *Mensch*," were the last words that my father said to me before he was led to the death trains and disappeared forever. We were standing on the *Appelplatz* assembly place in the Concentration Camp Krakow-Plaszow one early morning in mid-May 1944. Moments later, in complete clarity about his fate, he would be led off to the box cars of the train that was to take him and others selected by the Nazi doctor to Auschwitz. There he would be murdered in the gas chambers.

I tried to give him the only possession I had – a small piece of bread I carried with me – as an expression of hope for his survival even in Auschwitz. He said, "You keep it; I will not need it anymore; I do not care to live. I have lost everything and if I live another ten years I will eat another ton of potatoes." He pushed the bread back to me. It was the last time I saw him. Tears blurred my vision. As he was marched off he turned his head in my direction and saw me, his eldest son, and one of the few survivors of his entire family for the last time.

For the rest of my life I treasured this legacy, my fathers' blessing that I become a mensch. I tried to live by my father's words and to fulfill his teaching as best I could. I do not think that even with all my efforts I came close to achieving the level he had achieved in his short life. May his memory be blessed and may he be remembered by us the living to serve as a warning for generations to come. We must guard against racial policies like those propagated by the Nazis which killed my father at the age of fifty-two, my mother at age forty, my sister and brother at the threshold of their adult lives and my youngest brother when he was still a child.

With my father's departure I was now left alone in this world. The pages that follow serve as a memorial to my family and the millions of victims of Hitler's racial policies of extermination. My account begins with my growing up in the town of Krosno in Southern Poland before World War II. It follows my odyssey through the tragic years of the Holocaust. It ends with the immediate post-liberation period and my immigration to the United States, my adopted country and the land of the free – a country and a people to whom my gratitude is inexpressible.

Jewish survivors of the Holocaust share one thing in common. With very rare exceptions survivors lost either their entire family or nearly their entire family. Their stories often differ only on a few factors, such as where they were imprisoned, whether concentration camp or labor camp, and under whom the camp was administered, whether the SS, military, or civilian governments. The survivors' views of Germans and other nationalities also differ depending on their experiences.

It has been my experience, for example, that those who were sent to Siberia tend to have more negative views of Germans than those who remained in Germany. Having escaped from Poland and the invading German armies to Soviet Russia at the start of the war, these Jews, who ended up in Siberia, often never met Germans. They blame Germany for uprooting them and lack any positive experiences with ordinary Germans to counter-balance their negative view. Because I lived and worked among many ordinary good Germans during the war – especially those I encountered at the air base in our home town where I lived for a year – my feelings about them are much more benign. I was also fortunate to live toward the end of the war in the camp run by Oskar Schindler who was helped in his humanitarian efforts by his wife Emilie. I have thus learned one of the lessons of the Holocaust: The good and the bad in mankind cuts across all nationalities and institutions.

My life experiences have given me a great appreciation for the freedoms that the United States grants and protects. I hope that as you read this account you will come to a greater appreciation of the freedoms safe-guarded by the Bill of Rights as well. To paraphrase the great Polish-Lithuanian poet, Adam Mickiewicz: *"Freedom, you are like health. How precious to hold you. Only one can know who has lost you."*

- Alexander White

PART I

Krosno: My Home Before the War

Krosno

Krosno Synagogue

Krosno Rynek – before the war

Krosno: My Home Before the War

Just before World War II the population of Krosno, Poland was approximately 18,000, mostly Roman Catholic. Jews had not been allowed to live in towns (except surrounding villages) – or to own any land – until the Austrian annexation of the area as part of the Austro-Hungarian Empire. By the 1930s there were about 36-38 million people in all of Poland and only about ten percent were Jews. Krosno, meaning "loom," where I was born and raised is about 100 miles southeast of the great city of Krakow and recently celebrated 1,000 years of existence. It is in the south close to the Dukla Pass across the Carpathian Mountains that separate Poland from pre-war Czechoslovakia. All of the towns in the area have central squares but Krosno is known as "Little Krakow" because of its beautiful arcade so much like the arcades of that great city.

My mother's father, Chaim Hirsch Platner and his wife Mala were among the first Jews to settle in Krosno. Before World War I they were in the firewood and coal business and later they changed to glazing, glass beveling and framing. They had four sons and two daughters. My mother Leah was the youngest and married my father Mendel Bialywlos from Dabrowa-Tarnowska, a town about 50 miles away.

My father was taken into the glazing business in partnership with my grandfather Chaim Hirsch and my uncle Joseph Platner. Everyone in my mother's family married and lived in Krosno except for her oldest brother Jacob who lived in Czechoslovakia which was also part of the Austro-Hungarian Empire. They had big families – from two to eight children in each. I was blessed to have so many cousins, aunts and uncles living right in the same home town. In those days people did not migrate as they do today. Our family, like most others of the time was very close-knit. Under normal circumstances most of us would be born, marry and die in the same town sometimes even in the same house.

Grandfather Chaim was born and raised in a mountain village.[1] I remember his long white beard, an even longer pipe reaching to his thighs, and a limp caused when he fell off a ladder while building the Rabbi's *Sukkah*, the ceremony structure – a kind of tent *Sukkot*. He had a talent for working with wood and use to make for us all kinds of toys - guns shooting out little wooden bullets, decorated canes, *dreidels* for Hannukah *Haman* noise-makers for the reading of the *Megilat.* Esther on Purim sounded each time *Haman's* name is mentioned. For the *Simchat Torah*, "Joy of the Torah," holiday he made us children small flags with an ark in the center that opened up and revealed miniature Torahs inside.

He built the wooden wall sections for the assembly of ours and the rabbi's *sukkah*. They were wonderfully decorated. He made great pens out of goose feathers with different tips for his own beautiful calligraphic handwriting. He created the *Mizrach*, an eastern wall hanging depicting the holy temple to remind us of the destruction of the temple and to pray toward the east and Jerusalem. I remember one of the inscriptions: "Man concerns himself with losing money and shows no concern for losing days. Moneys do not help and days do not return." He kept all of his official papers including correspondence with Austrian authorities neatly

---

[1] Probably Bukowsko, according to one of my older cousins.

wrapped and bound in old drawers in the cellar. All was lost when we were forced out during the Holocaust.

My cousin Moniek, Sarah's son, claims that my grandfather was an angry man and that he was displeased with their family.[2] Another cousin, now from Israel, explained that Chaim disapproved of Aunt Sarah's youngsters because they were not religious enough. Perhaps he disliked them because they ran around with "gentile kids," smoked on the Sabbath, and secretly bought non-kosher kielbasa and ate it in hiding. They also did not fast on Yom Kippur, joking that they had to eat to have the strength to fast.

Grandmother Mala, Chaim's wife, came from the small *Shtetl* 'little town' of Frysztak. A tough little lady who ran the show, she was known as "Mala in the boots." She was, in fact, very tiny, but clearly the Matriarch. When my cousin David (also Aunt Sarah's son) a mechanic and tool and die maker needed a job she went to see the mayor. Patting the mayor on the back, she told him to intervene with the head of the industrial concern TEPEGE which didn't take in any Jewish workers. She simply assumed that he should arrange for her grandson to get a position there. TEPEGE was involved in the production and repair of oil well drilling equipment and had the best paying jobs in town but not for Jews. David did get the job but he had to work on the Sabbath.

Grandmother Mala was a healer. She would put on *banki* 'cups' for colds or *pijawki* 'leaches' for bloodletting – better said, "bloodsuck-

___
[2] Sarah was my mother's sister

3

ing." I still remember once when I had a fever and a swollen face.[3] She took a handful of flax, lit it, and rotated it over my face intoning a sort of "chasing-evil-away" chant. It must have worked because I recovered fully without sequel. Until I was an older kid I wore the red band around my wrist that Grandmother had put on me to keep away the evil spirits.

She was also the counselor for the Jewish women of Krosno. On Sabbath afternoons she read to a group of women from the "*Tzena Ure-nah*" which was the Yiddish translation of the Old Testament. And she was full of wise little sayings which I remember well. When a woman complained about gaining weight, protesting that she was not eating all that much, Grandmother told her, "From skinny noodles you don't get a broad *tuches*!" To those who were mixing in their daughter-in-laws affairs she would say, "Two pillows don't need a third head." Another saying which has special significance for me now as I reflect on the dark days that awaited all of us, "You can't board up the world with boards." I have always felt that she was actually saying, "You can't shut out reality."

And she was feared by my cousins. Cousin Mark (still another of Aunt Sarah's sons) was a rough character that used to beat up anyone who got in his way – me included. Grandmother Mala went after him with a broom screaming as he ran away, "If I catch you I will pull your *Pulka* 'leg' out if you dare touch him (me) again!"

Grandmother Mala was a *Chasid* 'follower' of the Rabbi of Muka-chewo[4] of Hungary. Even in winter she would put on her boots and travel by a horse-drawn sled to see him and ask for advice. My cousins told a

---

[3] I would guess it was most likely Erysipelas, a streptococcal skin infection.
[4] *Munkacher* in Yiddish

story about when Mala's son, (my uncle) Abraham was to be drafted into the Austrian army where he would have to eat non-kosher food and shave his beard; Grandmother took him to the *Munkatscher* rabbi for help. The Rabbi told her "Mala! Don't worry, they will not take him." Whereupon the rabbi took his long pipe and hit Abe on the shoulder. Abe got a *Gibbus* 'hunchback.' Of course the army would not take a hunch back and everything was OK. The rabbi had performed a miracle. But when the time came to marry Abe off, nobody wanted a hunchback for a husband. So Mala went back to the rabbi. The rabbi said again, "Mala don't worry! Whereupon he hit Abe with his pipe on the other shoulder and it straightened Abe out.

And there was another story about Mala. Before WWI when the family was in the firewood business Mala and a few men would go to the villages buying up wood. Once in the home of a peasant there was a fire. Everyone but Mala ran out. When the men peeked in through the smoke-filled window to look for her there she was, standing still, not moving at all. After the fire was extinguished she came out. When they ask her why she didn't run, she said, "Once when I visited the Rabbi he told me, "If anything should ever happen to you Mala just stay there and don't run." So she stood there and was saved.[5]

I was grandmother Mala's favored grandson. She claimed I had an *Eisernem Kopf* 'iron brain' due to my rapid comprehension and memory. Already by age three or four, I could recite the prayers and sections of the bible by heart after just one or two readings. She thought that I was going

---

[5] These days my stockbroker is offering me the same advice: "Stay the course."

to grow up to be the greatest *Gaon* 'super rabbi' in Poland. "Oy!" My cousins said to my kids, "Would grandmother Mala be disappointed if she saw your father today! He is not only not a rabbi but a *Goy*, 'a gentile' who doesn't keep Kosher, eats pork and even married a woman whose mother wasn't Jewish which according to Jewish law made my wife non-Jewish.

More recollections . . . Thursday nights Grandmother Mala and my mother would start baking *Challah* - rolls and sweets for the Sabbath. They worked until about two a.m. and that glorious smell kept me awake in bed. The next day for an early lunch we dined on *tinkiechts* which means 'dunkings.' We dunked the rolls in calf's liver and sautéed onions with gravy. It was heavenly. Even nowadays I often sauté onions either with liver or another meat and gravy using white rolls for dunking - incidentally, sautéed onions and white bread without any meat or gravy tastes just as good. A Polish non-Jewish friend, a neurosurgeon from Warsaw, and his Italian brother-in-law were visiting once in our home. I had just sautéed some onions and I saw that their taste buds were salivating. I served them big plates of the onions with matzah and they devoured it. They even wanted my recipe.[6]

Friday afternoons and the days before a holiday were busy. The men hurried to the *Schvits* 'Finnish steam bath, sauna, and bathhouse' to clean up for the Sabbath which started at sundown. As the first star appeared signaling the beginning of the Sabbath, mother and grandmother lit

---

[6] It reminded me of a recent ad showing a Native American in full attire devouring a corned beef sandwich on rye bread. The inscription read: "You don't have to be Jewish to like Rosen's rye."

the candles and covered their eyes in prayer. We men went to prayer services around the corner at the rabbi's *schtibel* 'private prayer room.' I remember my father, always late, barely managing to shine his boots and
change his attire for the Sabbath.

In Krosno you didn't need a calendar because you could smell the
upcoming holiday. The aroma of *gefillte* fish and parsley in the soup pen-
etrated even the street air. At home after the evening service we sat down
at the candlelit table, sang the prayer greeting the Sabbath and sanctified
the wine. Everybody got a sip. My father wouldn't spend any money on
real wine. His so-called wine consisted of grapes ground up the day before with water added. Grandfather Chaim had made a special contraption
which consisted of a large box lined with a heavy sheet metal on the inside
and a lighter sheet-metal cover. The box fit over the gas burners on the
stove. The women would prepare the fish for the Sabbath dinner and
Tscholent for Saturday. The pots of food that needed baking or to be kept
hot were placed in it just before the Sabbath, the burners were put on very
low flame and the box was covered and left until dinner the following day.
It was a sort of slow crock cooking that made everything taste wonderful.

The *gefillte* fish was followed by chicken soup with either farfel or
noodles and then came chicken and compote. In between the courses we
sang religious songs. After the first slice of the *challah*, my father substituted it with cheaper rye bread in order to "not raise us on expensive white
bread." Sometimes when it came to serving the meat mother found only
one leg in the pot. She would say, "This was apparently a one-legged
chicken!" It didn't take much to guess who had stolen the leg out of the

pot. . . . *"Who stole the Kishka?"* It was I – the *fresser* 'glutton.'
You've probably heard that old song.

Saturday, Sabbath morning, the streets were empty. The stores in
the center of town, mostly Jewish, were closed. After the prayers were
intoned on arising, *"How wonderful your tents of Jacob,"* and others we
sometimes went to the *schvitz* which was still hot from the day before.
We did not reheat the stones on the Sabbath. There we usually found
many others including our Gentile teacher Gruszka enjoying the bath. It
was a room with bleachers and heated rocks over which we poured water
from time to time to generate the steam. At the top, the heat was extreme.
You had to go up there with a bucket of cold water and inhale from it.
Pine brooms were available for flogging your back which made you even
hotter. It was supposed to be good for your health. After the hot *schvitz*
you ran down to the cold ritual *Mikvah* 'pool' which was connected to a
very cold well. There was a "hot" *Mikvah* in one of the rooms where the
younger boys loved to sit and masturbate. It was rather unsightly, not to
mention unsanitary with clumps of ejaculate floating in the water and it
smelled accordingly. On weekdays young orthodox women went in to the
hot *Mikvah* for their ritual post-menstruation immersion as kids peeked in
through a venting window which opened on the top. Schmuel Chaim, an
elderly Jew with a sense of humor used to joke that even if you threw a
barrel of perfume in there it would still stink.

After the *schvitz* on Saturday we went to the morning service
which usually lasted until noon. The men wore prayer shawls under their
coats and handkerchiefs around their necks. You were not allowed to carry anything as it was considered "work" and the Sabbath was for rest. But

acting as though what you carried was part of your clothing was permitted. I've always thought of it as "fooling the Almighty."

The bible says, "You shall not burn a fire on the day of Sabbath" so all candles were lit before the start of the Sabbath. You were not even allowed to touch the candleholders as a precaution against being tempted to light the candles. Once I tried to show that I could touch the holder without lighting the candle. I got hit in the face by my father. When I questioned him about the prayer for the rebuilding of the holy temple in Jerusalem and once again bringing sacrifice there as in ancient times, I asked, "Would it not be wild to nowadays sacrifice lambs at an altar in the temple?" The answer was simple: "You don't question the Torah, it applies to all ages and all times." The answer did not satisfy me but I did not pursue it any further.

On the way home from prayers gentile children sometimes threw stones at us Jews. My cousin Mark would hide and when the kids started throwing at his father he'd jump up and beat the hell out of them. Mark was a rough character. During WWII he served in the Polish army under General Anders. When he was stationed in Egypt he became bored and volunteered for the front line at Monte Cassino in Italy. The sergeant, who liked him, took him to the Field Hospital to visit all the casualties who were missing arms and legs. He asked him, "Do you want this?" My cousin stopped volunteering for the front.

On Saturday afternoons the women took us children to the City Park. We played, caught frogs in the small pond and used the swings. The men took a walk into the Market Square and talked about news and the world situation. My father was usually the central figure with everyone else tilting his head to hear his view. He was an "authority" on the news because he read everything he could get his hands on and went frequently to Dr. Dym's library. When I was older, I was allowed to be with my father both at the library and at these meetings in the central square.

Grandfather Chaim and Grandmother Mala lived with us in the two rooms behind our shop. Actually, we lived with them. It was a crowded place. In one very small room with two beds the four of us children slept head to foot per bed. It accommodated only a small table with two chairs and a wardrobe. The bigger room just behind the shop served as a bedroom for everyone else as well as the dining room and the kitchen. On top of that when relatives came to visit like when red-bearded Uncle Enoch from Jaslo came with his two sons for the holidays we children slept on straw sacks on the floor so they could have our two beds. Our little house was truly the gathering place for the family.

My Grandfather on my father's side, Abraham Bialywlos, was a cobbler in Dabrowa, Tarnowska about 50 miles northwest of Krosno. His wife (my grandmother) had been killed by shrapnel during World War I. Besides my father, there was Alter Bialywlos, the oldest brother, Samuel, the youngest and a childless sister and her husband. Alter had four daughters and two sons who lived in Jaslo which was only about 17 miles from Krosno. Uncle Sam had one or two children and lived in Gorlice, a small town not far to the west, also near the border with Czechoslovakia.

Grandfather Abraham would sit at a low cobbler stool repairing shoes. He also had a long gray beard like Grandfather Chaim but didn't smoke. He lived in one room with my aunt and her husband who sold fruit from a stand in the market. I remember on Friday afternoons they

10

would come home from the market with leftover fruit. With no time to prepare it for the Sabbath they would rinse it and throw it with the peels on in a pot to boil.

Without a mother and with a father who was very poor and always working my father Mendel essentially grew up in the home of Rabbi Dov Weidenfeld the famous rabbi in Dabrowa. This rabbi looked traditional but he was not steeped in the Chasidic traditions. He was more scholarly. I heard my father tell my mother that the rabbi had teachers from Vienna who came to his house in Dabrowa. I have often wondered if my father's enlightened ideas and apparent secular education was picked up through visits to the rabbi's place.

Once my father took me to Dabrowa and we stayed at the rabbi's cottage-style spacious home with a beautiful garden full of fresh flowers and vegetables. Today I can still remember a Sabbath afternoon there and taste the vegetable and challah sandwich. The rabbi examined me in the Scriptures and was very impressed that at age four I could recite the prayers, read the Torah and even chant the *Megilah* (story of Esther) by heart. So now I was not only recognized as a super *Gaon* 'great scholar' by Grandmother Mala but also by the famous and revered rabbi, author of commentaries to the Torah. My father was visibly proud.

On our way home to Krosno we stopped in the larger town of Tarnow where my father had a cousin. The family had a tiny kiosk for selling candy. I had to use the toilet which had a central water tank with a pull-chain for flushing. This was completely new to me. We had an outhouse – indoor plumbing didn't come to Krosno until the early 1930's. I pulled on the handle and heard the water rushing down loudly. I pulled again and again hoping it would stop running. So I kept on pulling, I was sure I had broken something. But I didn't give up. My father eventually found me still yanking on the chain determined to make it work.

At a store owned by someone name Quadratstein my father bought himself a round velvet hat and for my mother a sweater with maroon and alternating navy-blue stripes. His purchase for her was exceptional because machine-made sweaters were expensive. It was much more common to buy the wool and have a lady come to the house, measure us and make not only sweaters but all of our clothing. Labor was cheap.

My father had learned the craft and the business of glazing when he married my mother. He was given 20 percent and together with my uncle Joseph owned the largest building in town. I remember once browsing among the carefully sorted and bound papers kept in our drawer and seeing the purchasing record of that building bought from an attorney named Abderman. It quoted $33,000. They also acquired a warehouse with a train track connected to it at the railroad station. More than half of the warehouse was rented out to a large food cooperative named Spolem and the smaller part was used for our glass business.

As the industrialization of Poland commenced in the 1930s a new rolled-glass factory was built which for the first time gave competition to the only rolled glass plants in Szczakowa and Zabkowice, both owned by a Belgian company. There were other multiple glass factories; however, they were of the hand-blown plate variety. The latter was cheap but one saw multiple faces in it; it was wavy, varied widely in thickness and was more difficult to cut and work with. It could not be used for mirrors. Nowadays this hand-made variety has become "art" glass and costs consider-

12

ably more as it is labor intensive. Because of the intense competition between the rolled glass companies prices dropped to the bottom. It was clear that one of them would have to go broke at those below-cost prices. My father and uncle decided to stock-up the warehouse with glass in anticipation of a price rise.

My father was extremely hard working. He would get up while it was still dark and go out to the wholesale warehouse where the buyers from the surrounding towns and villages were already waiting with their horse-drawn wagons to get the deliveries. Then he came to the shop in town and stayed busy all day. At night he would stay up late doing the business books, chanting as he calculated the balances. He was always busy with something, and expected his children to be so too. The rule was, you must never be sitting around.

When we were busy in the shop my mother and Aunt Dworah (Joseph's wife) would help out. My mother knew how to cut glass and glaze as well. Not infrequently when the shop was so busy that the customers spilled into our living space - even if my mother was busy cooking - my father would cut off the gas to the stove burners and insist that she leave everything and come to help with the customers.

He didn't like to spend money on anything he considered frivolous. Mother used to hide a bar of chocolate or an orange for us kids so he would not see her spending money on such "luxuries." He liked to buy second hand clothes and just have the tailor turn them inside out. I remember once when he bought me new shoes from the peasants who brought their wares to the *Jarmark* 'monthly market on a Monday.' The shoes were homemade and cheap. The tip of the shoes was cardboard as was the inner layer of the soles. After one rain they fell apart.

On the Sabbath when my mother served home-made baked flour *challah* he would give each of us only a slice and then switch to whole grain rye bread which was cheaper. He would say, "I am not going to raise my kids on white bread and luxuries," recalling the hunger in his home during WWI. He wanted us to be able to weather tough times should they come. He would buy a huge sack of flour during the harvest because he could get it for less instead of going to the store every other day to buy a pound or so for making noodles. My mother spent many Sundays making noodles galore and storing them in bags.[7]

I remember how much I liked to help out in the corner kitchen. I frequently dried the dough and cut the noodles. I also loved to go with mother to the market to buy chickens and geese[8] and take them for ritual slaughter by the Schochet. I would pluck the feathers, cut off the thick fatty skin and render the fat. The curdles and goose fat on a piece of rye bread tasted delicious. The remainder of the fat we stored in the cellar for year round use. In the spring just before Passover we would go to the market with two pails and fill them up with eggs for the holiday. And in the summer we would buy buckets full of raspberries for making syrup. After they were boiled and the syrup pressed out of them we children played with the raspberries forming them into bright pink "snowballs."

We lived frugally but not so Uncle Joseph, my father's business partner. My father was thin; Uncle Joseph was fat. He built himself a

---

[7] The rats helped themselves to the flour too!
[8] In the winter at Christmas time geese were cheap.

house with four bedrooms, modern bathrooms and a modern kitchen on Francziszkanska Street next to the Franciscan church. He wore a coat lined with minks with the tails hanging out. Uncle Joseph suffered from migraine headaches. He treated himself by cutting off the head of a large black radish and pasting it to his forehead. It looked as if it were growing there. He occasionally invited congregants to his home for schnapps and hors d'oeuvres after services. My Uncle Chaim Fruhman often told the story that my father and he were asked to help out with the serving. My uncle took a schnapps and a cookie and asked my father why he would not do the same. My father's response, "What I would not do at my home I will not do in somebody else's."

Of course my father didn't drink either. On one occasion he re-fused to take us children to our cousin's wedding which everyone else at-tended claiming, "They don't need another mouth to feed there." When we protested he said, "Just imagine that you were there already and you are now back home." Not that he wasn't generous on occasion. He lent money to Uncle Chaim to buy provisions for his store. At the same time, however, he complained to my mother that he wished Uncle Chaim were not such a "spender." When people asked him why he worked so hard and spent so little he would answer that he was doing it for the sake of us children so we wouldn't have to. People used to say he was saving *kischka* 'gut' money by saving on food.

But what he valued mostly was education. Whenever he had a lit-tle free time on weekends he would go over to Dr. Dym's library and read German and Polish periodicals. He also read Goethe, Schiller, Heine and Lessing. And he forced us to sit with him and listen to his recitation of

15

their poems and books. He would buy old newspapers by the bundle and read the editorials. If he noticed us sitting idle for even a moment he would pull out Spinoza, Aristotle and Socrates. I was frequently bored with it and would have rather played outside. As I was dozing off out of boredom he would wake me up by hitting my shoulder with his fist. Eventually he had to give up.

In political and world news he was the expert. Whenever we went for a walk or to the synagogue people would surround us to hear the latest news and my father's opinion about it. During the Sino-Japanese and later the Abyssinian war even I knew the position of the forces and cities that were occupied.

Today I still believe that my father was the first person to diagnose what is now called GERD (gastro esophageal reflux disease). And what he did demonstrated for me its now-known frequent relation to asthma. It was one night when I went to bed after eating. I was reading in bed when I suddenly started coughing and wheezing. My mother was quite con-cerned but my father said simply, "It serves him right he *fresses* too much." He had me get out of bed and walk around. My coughing attack cleared up. Another time I developed a skin rash with small blisters. I am certain now that it was chicken pox. My father took a handful of kosher salt and rubbed it into my skin. Of course it burned like hell and broke the blister but it also cured the itch!

By almost everyone my father was considered fair and understand-ing. People came to him for advice and for settling of disagreements. And the workers and clients preferred to deal with him rather than Uncle Joseph. Uncle Joseph would tease and joke with them before paying them

16

for their day's work. My father would tell him, "Joseph, these people have families pay them their due and let them go home." He was also more liberal than the Rabbi in town when it came to religious matters such as judging whether a chicken with a nail in its gullet or an egg with a drop of blood in it was kosher. He felt sorry for the women who would then have to sell their non-kosher food to a Gentile for a marked loss.

He practiced strict orthodoxy to be certain but was quite liberal where earning a living was concerned. I remember an episode when a number of orthodox Jews went to a widow whose son worked in a factory where he had to work on the Sabbath.   The son was the only earner. My father admonished the people to leave the woman alone. There was also the case with my cousin David, a tool and die maker in the TEPEGE factory where he also had to work on the Sabbath. My father understood and accepted that reality. I also remember a barber newly arrived in Krosno who was one of the rare converts to Christianity. Orthodox Jews broke his windows and my father was adamant in his stand against such intolerance. He hated inhumane behavior.

I remember a man by the name of Hezekiah who made a meager living pushing a wheelbarrow going from house to house collecting metal junk which he would sell to the junkyard of Mr. Kalb by weight. His clothes were torn and with his wife and two children he lived in a single room. Some kids would make fun of him as they did of Chaskel Parech and other handicapped people. One time I happened to be with a group, some of whom chased and made fun of Hezekiah. His wife Revalah knew that going to the fathers of those kids was useless because they wouldn't pay her any attention. She came to my father and told him that I was with

them. Without asking me any questions he gave me a terrible beating.
"How would you like to be in Hezekiah's place and be treated with such
disrespect?" In truth I had been a bystander; I wouldn't have dared do
what they did. Crying, I protested the unjust punishment. My father said
simply, "You shouldn't have been with such kids." In my father's eyes I
was guilty by association.

I remember Revalah so well, the tiny woman with horribly bowed
legs and her two sons. One was Motele who was my schoolmate and very
shrewd. The other was Sanaleh who was small, also severely bowlegged,
and had hands with very short fingers. Sanaleh was a sweet likeable boy
who used his stubby fingers, especially the thumb, to draw amazing
sketches reminiscent of Chagal. There were little houses grouped into villages and *shtetls* quite naïve and distorted. I really believe that he would
have been another Chagal had he survived. Tragically he and three other
handicapped people were taken out one day in 1942 when the Gestapo
wanted some Jews for shooting. The head of the Judenrat decided to let
them take the handicapped instead of healthy people. Of course they all
died and that same Judenrat headman later perished in the Holocaust.

Reform Judaism which had its origin in Germany in the 19th century was a copy of the Protestantism that resulted from the Catholic Re-
formation. It was this form of Judaism that would later be brought to
America by the Jewish-German immigrants. It was essentially unknown
in Eastern Europe where Orthodox Judaism prevailed with its maintenance
of strict Kosher rules, synagogues and private worship places, *schtibels*,
Chasidic groups and a variety of Zionist-oriented groups, the religious and
secular abounded. Orthodox Jewish men grew beards and sideburns – ei-

18

ther long corkscrew-curls that hung down past their shoulders or shorter ones which they hid behind their ears. They dressed in long black or gray coats (*caftans*) and black hats. Under their shirts were a garment '*tassel*' with prescribed fringes '*tzitzes*' and a belt-like black cord worn around the waist especially during the prayers to separate the upper clean part of the body from the lower unclean part.

They prayed loudly, weaving their bodies back and forth or in circles, immersed and in contact with the angels in heaven. They were absent from this world for the duration.[9] On the Sabbath and on holidays the *caftans* were made of shiny materials and their hats were lined with fur tails. The men attended synagogue service morning and evening and spent hours studying the scriptures and commentaries. To the gentiles these orthodox Jews were a curiosity out of the Middle Ages. Their wives wore wigs over shaved heads and were frequently the breadwinners while their husbands remained immersed in the Word of God.

The Jews in Krosno and in all of Poland were small shopkeepers, craftsmen of all trades and professionals. Except for the professionals, most of them were poor by today's standards. They were supported by *Landsmanschaft* associations organized by relatives who had left their respective towns to emigrate to America, and other Jewish-American organizations. Non-Jews thought that all Jews were rich and were hiding money in their pillowcases. The truth was that most barely scraped out a living.

---

[9] In our Schtibel there was a man named Berish Blumenfeld who made all kinds of grimaces during prayers, raising his arms frequently as if to catch the angels by their feet.

They dreamed of immigrating to Palestine and even more so to America, that free "golden" land with all its opportunities. Unfortunately for most it remained only a dream. The lucky ones who managed to get visas and settle in the U.S. sometimes returned to their *shtetls* 'small towns' completely metamorphosed in modern dress, clean-shaven or with trimmed beards and bringing gifts and money for their families and relatives. Many abandoned their wives in the *shtetls* and married modern American ladies. The children from the new families attended American colleges and universities and became professionals or scholars as did other immigrants. We see the same today with the new arrivals from South America, Asia, Africa and Eastern Europe.[10]

Chaim Weitzman, the first President of the new Israel, once said, "The Jews carry the seeds of Anti-Semitism with them wherever they go." That does seem to be true. Our presence in almost every country in the world has historically made us scapegoats for so many ills. Accusations are outrageous and absurd. Coming from anti-Semites: "The Plague and AIDS were invented and spread by Jews to kill Gentiles and dominate the world." More recently, "The drop of the value of the money in Malaysia and the Japanese recession? Who else but the Jews." Preposterous.[11]

---

[10] We immigrants are the lucky ones and we owe this nation a great debt. Where else in the world can you be as free as we are in America in the pursuit of happiness for yourself and your family.

[11] Even in Spain where the Jews had all been eliminated or forced out by the Inquisition in 1492 there were rude jokes surrounding the Spanish Civil War nearly 400 years later. The saying went: "A republican Spaniard asked his adversary, "Why are we killing each other? Aren't we all Spaniards?" The answer: "It's all because of the Jews because if we had Jews in Spain we would be killing them instead of each other!"

As we now well know, Europe, especially Eastern Europe was infested with Anti-Semitism. New Poland during the inter-war period had a democratic constitution but it is one thing to have a written document and another to abide by it. During the first half of the 1930s when Marshall Pilsudski, the Polish hero of Independence, ruled the country in a benevolent dictatorial way (a la DeGaulle in France) Jewish life flourished. Anti-Semitism though present was kept under control. With Pilsudski's demise in May 1935 and the ascent to power of General Smigly-Rydz the rightist anti-Semitic organizations came out in the open. Anti-Jewish laws were proposed and some were passed. Graffiti with slogans such as "Jews to Palestine," "Out with Jews," "Kill Jews," and "Don't buy from Jews" were seen on walls. There continued to be accusations just as there had been in the Middle Ages when it was alleged that Jews killed Christian youngsters in order to use their blood for Passover Matzos known as the "Protocols of Zion" and other such ridiculous accusations. And even a few pogroms (massacres) were held – portent of things to come. Gentile students returning to their towns on summer recess organized boycotts of Jewish stores and prevented buyers from entering. They organized attacks on Jewish sports clubs, often planning and coordinating these activities in Christian student club meetings in their own churches.

In public grade school I myself suffered enough indignities at the hands of some of the kids so as to be afraid to go to the latrine because a gentile classmate would turn around and urinate on me. On occasion the boy next to me would pass gas, plug his nose and loudly proclaim, "The Jew stinks." The other children would then move away. I was beaten up a few times. In the winter they waited outside, threw me to the ground and rubbed my face with snow so that I arrived home with a swollen face.

My mother complained to Mr. Gruszka our biology teacher who was a very decent man. He called the kid out and admonished him "You are eating Jewish bread at home, your father works in a Jewish factory! How could you do that?" But, in truth, it wasn't much fun going to public school. The trouble reflected in my grades where I had mostly passing grades except in citizenship and music. Later on in the secondary school with older students this was not the case and I made good grades. I even jumped a year ahead and was exempt from final exams.

Where do children learn such behavior? It must be at home of course from their parents but it is reinforced by their peers. The better students didn't do these unkind things but the truth be told they also didn't come to my assistance. They were indifferent. Sadly, such indifference would only increase and would be manifest in the worldwide indifference displayed by the vast majority during the Holocaust. My teachers were usually kind but there was no teaching of tolerance as a social more. Poland had substantial minorities – German, mostly in the western parts and Ukrainian in the southeastern – but being Christian they didn't suffer such indignities.

Overall, the relationship of Jews and Gentiles was for the most part one of peaceful coexistence. Social interaction other than for business was infrequent. Since the majority of Jews were orthodox and the Church was basically an unfriendly institution this formal separation was quite evident in a country as rigidly Catholic as Poland.

I remember an episode when I was helping my father to glaze some broken windows in a convent. The cleaning woman began chasing me around with her broom, yelling. "You Christ-killer!" "Get out of here!" She did not stop until a nun intervened. Another time I was walking along the road with my uncle when a driver in a horse-pulled wagon tried to force us off the side of the road into a ditch and began whipping my uncle with his horsewhip. My uncle complained to his boss and to the Police. At least this particular perpetrator spent two days in jail.

Another time we were to do some glazing at an old refinery and they sent their bus driver to pick us up. My father, my aunt's brother and I sat, each holding several plates of glass. Suddenly and I am certain purposefully the driver swerved the bus left and right in order to throw us. We fell with the glass breaking many of the plates and we were cut as well. I do not intend that you the reader should construe these incidences of cruelty to apply to all Polish gentiles, by no means. Nevertheless it is a fact that Jews have learned over and over to adapt to such treatment through the centuries since the Diaspora. But we have also thrived economically, culturally and even socially. In Poland and in Krosno our Jewish community had such self-help organizations as "assistance to the sick" whereby the women brought kosher meals to the sick in the hospital, a free loan society that lent money to needy Jews without interest, its own burial society and many other vital community organizations.

When I was only three I started *Cheder* 'Jewish preschool.'[12] The teacher was Moshe Faiwel a short man with a black beard and curled peios

---

[12] A teacher was called Rebbe or Melamed.

'sideburns.' He and his wife the Rebecin and their two sons, both tailors who wore modern clothes and shaved their premature beards[13] lived in a small low house very near the river Wislok. In the spring whenever the river overflowed, water entered the house.

The Rebbe had a Belfer 'helper' who worked for room and board and whose function among others was to pick up the kids at their homes and lead them in pairs and holding hands to the Cheder and back home. We walked barefooted in the summer to save on soles. Cheder was an all-day affair. In winter we never got home until it was already dark and the Belfer used a candle lantern.

The Belfer slept in the kitchen inside a box with a lid which served also as a bench. The house had one room with a small kitchen where the whole family lived and there was a larger teaching room which also con-tained an oven. At the head of the table sat the Rebbe with the Belfer and we pupils were seated on benches along the side. The Rebbe kept a basket with long sticks nearby in case we had trouble learning the weekly section of the bible by Friday. He would wave one stick continuously as he taught. Those in the basket served as reserves. If you didn't know your stuff you had to bend over and get a few whips. Sometimes he had you drop your pants. If you misbehaved badly the Belfer would put you in one of the Rebecin's old dresses and an old hat with feathers. You were placed on top of the stove and shamed before the other kids. He had you stand there while the other kids made fun. This punishment, called a

---

[13] Neither did they have peios.

peckel was the worst. I was fortunate. I never received any kind of punishment at Cheder.

Outside was a small playground with a few tables and benches where we would play or eat our brought-from-home lunches. Some parents brought warm food. I watched with jealously as they begged their children to eat. In our home if I ever got mad and threatened a hunger strike my father would simply take my plate away and say, "He is as hungry as a miller's chicken. He will eat when he gets hungry." There was no subsequent begging to eat. Of course I would steal down into the cellar and stuff my pockets with the fruit stored there. I would also sometimes threaten my mother with renting myself out to Uncle Abraham who made wine and would let me take a suck on the hose to start the transfer from one barrel to another. He was also less strict with his children.

The door into the Cheder house was low and most adults had to bend down to enter it. Outside a ladder led up to the attic where the rabbi raised a rooster and chickens. The eggs were collected every morning and the chickens roamed around the playground all day. They were fed old bread soaked in water. Above us on the hill leading from the river into the inner town was Mr. Bendet's Cheder. Older students studied there. One memory which has stayed with me was a fire that broke out at Mr. Bendet's. We at Moshe Faiwel's were sent home. It was dark and the fire wagon arrived. Since it was a frame house it burned quickly. I remember the sparks cracking and flying all over and the giant flames going up into the black sky. For some time after I had horrible dreams. Since I was the best pupil at Cheder I was assigned to examine one of the other students before he advanced from the Hebrew alphabet called "*Aleph Bet*" to bible study. This was usually a celebrated event in the home of the graduating student. I was placed on top of the table opposite the candidate and asked him questions about the bible. Following his responses I would have to give him a pinch on his cheek and tell him, "Now that you are such a fine student you may start learning *Chumesh,* 'the Pentateuch.' After the ceremony everybody was served cookies and tea. Whenever I see that fellow who is now a physician living in New Jersey I remind him of this affair and the great jam his mother made.

I entered public grade school at the age of six, one year ahead of the mandatory age. My parents went to see the school director, Mr. Jagiello, and petitioned him to allow me to enter early since they thought I would not pass the first grade and would have to stay over. I could then catch up with the other kids. They were worried because we spoke exclusively Yiddish at home and I did not know Polish well. I surprised them. I could recite verbatim Mrs. Hewryczowa's first-grade verses and lectures even though I didn't understand them. And I could repeat and sing all the songs from school. I passed and was thus the youngest and smallest in class.

Every day after school and lunch at home I attended Hebrew Cheders and Yeshivas for more advanced studies such as the Talmud, the Prophets and other sacred texts. At thirteen I became Bar Mitzvah.[14] To not interfere with my secular education which my father deemed so important I attended the Yeshiva every morning from 6:00 until 7:30 am. I then ran home and changed from religious to secular attire and went to the pub-

---

[14] No big deal in the old country. Not like in the US where it's celebrated like a wedding.

lic school which was located on the street where we lived, Ordynacka Street. I still remember the briskness of the early morning air and the trumpeter who played from the steeple of the Parafialna Church. Even today it sounds in my ears.

In the more advanced Cheders each Rebbe had his own method of punishment. One had the habit of pulling hard on students' ears; others would hit them in the face whereas others like Moshe Faiwel had a whole selection of sticks for beating the students, usually on the behind. And some Rebbes hit students on the shoulder with their fists. To me they were sadists and nowadays they would be jailed for such abuse. We students would arrive early and sometimes bring garlic to rub the sticks so that they would dry out and break when someone got hit.

My cousin Mark, two years my senior, but in class with me, both in Cheder and public school was a rowdy kid who not only beat me up as I related earlier but organized clever escapes from the teacher. In the winter we studied by candlelight. Mark would have each one of us rub paraffin from the candle into the table sideboard and at his signal we were to light the board and yell, "fire." Then we were all to run out. Since I was the youngest the teacher had me sit first in the row. I was easy for the teacher to catch. I also had to absorb his saliva when he talked.

This particular Melamed was nicknamed "Foniu Mamzer." Foniu was a nickname for a Jew from the Russian occupied part of Poland and Mamzer stood for 'bastard.' This Melamed was as poor as a church mouse and was blessed (like the Fiddler on the Roof) with six daughters he was unable to feed. Every Friday the daughters would go from house to house and the people would give them some food for the Sabbath meal.

One would give a piece of fish, another a roll and so on, or they would have starved. Foniu's *caftan* was full of holes and I felt sorry for the family. The other Melameds were poor too but not like Foniu.

One summer the head of the Yeshiva in Krosno named *Kether Torah*,[15] Mr. Seligman took his three best pupils (me included) to his Rabbi of Radomsko who lived in Sosnowiec in western Poland. During the summer kids under twelve could ride free on the train as long as a paying adult accompanied them – but only two kids per traveler. Since we were three, one of us had to hide from the conductor. A different kid would be sent to the toilet each time the conductor would come by to check.

On the way we stopped in Krakow in the extremely orthodox part of the Jewish section called Kazimierz and went to the *schvitz* and ritual bathhouse there. The water in the *Mikvah* was like ice. It was the coldest experience I have ever had. I remember walking down to the well on the circular stairs and even though I was coming from the highest and hottest seat I could immerse my feet only up to my ankles before I had to run out. It felt like a knife was cutting my feet.

After breakfast in Krakow we took the train to Sosnowiec. We didn't have to hide on this part of the trip since there were many *Radomskier Chasidim* on the train going to the Rabbi's table for the Sabbath. When we arrived I was too hungry to wait for the Sabbath supper. Across the street I saw a store with the Hebrew inscription "Kosher" and inside a man with a beard and peios. I assumed that the place was kosher so I bought myself a salami sandwich. When the head of the Yeshiva found

---

[15] "Crown of the Torah"

out he bawled me out. How could I be so sure, even with the beard and peios, that it was a strict kosher place?

After the service at supper we were seated at a long table with the Chasidim. I remember that the Radomskier Rabbi was not a singer so he had one of the Chasidim sing the "Shalom Aleichem" greeting of the Sabbath. The Rabbi schlepped along. The next night the Rabbi's son-in-law examined us in the Talmud. Each one of us received a 10 grosches 'pennies' coin blessed by the Rabbi. On the way back home I traded the coin to another kid, Meilech First, for a box of chocolate from his father's store. The chocolate was rancid and tasted like soap.

This is a photo of our Krosno Rabbi. The Chasidic Rabbi Moshe Twerski of the famous Twerski Dynasty of Rabbis. It shows the Rabbi in the typical broad hat with some of his Chasidim in Iwonicz-zdroj, a resort town only 15 kilometers from Krosno.

The mechanical shop owned by Abraham Minz on Slowacki Street.
Altman is on the right and Weissman is on the left.

The Rabbi of our Jewish
congregation, Schmuel
Fuehrer. A known scholar.

This is my Uncle Abraham Platner, my mother's brother. He, together with his wife Hencia, daughters Sarah and Rachel, son Aaron, perished in the gas chamber of Belzec during the first "Umsied-lung" (resettlement) from Krosno in early summer of 1942. His oldest son, Joseph (called 'White Joe' because of his very blond, almost bleached white hair) was shot together with another cousin of mine nicknamed 'Red Joe' (because of his red hair) at the beginning of the war in September, 1939.

PART 2

The Gathering Clouds

Demeaning of Krosno Jews by the Nazis

The old Town of Krosno

Left to right: Szymon Guzik, Gershon Pasternack,
Mendel Schwebel (sole survivor), Naftali Monheit

My sister, Mania (the first one on the left) with friends. The last one on
the right is my cousin Ryvkah Platner, now Ryvkah Rand of Tel-Aviv,
a Siberian survivor. Ryvkah gave me this photo.

My sister Mania Bialywlos' school friends from Beyt Yaakov Hebrew School preparing to go on a summer outing. Mania is the second from the left. Most of them didn't survive.

The Gathering Clouds

I urge you dear reader not to view what I am about to describe as an historical document in the scholarly or academic sense. I am a physician by calling and not an historian. What follows is a story about the time period just before the war as I experienced it. I have added the information I gathered from reading Polish and Jewish periodicals of the day and from discussions I both heard and took part in as teenager in Krosno. I have also spent considerable time in my later life confirming my experience with research in German historical resources.

Although I was a youngster at the time, I and many other Jewish people in Poland followed closely all international events. We were markedly affected by whatever was happening and talked about current events intensively in the *schvitzes*, in the synagogue, in the streets and at home. People would approach me and ask, "Sender!" (My Yiddish first name, and abbreviation of Alexander, my Hebrew name) "Where are the Japanese now?" "The Chinese?"

During the Sino-Japanese war in the 1930s and when the Italians were in Africa, geography was my forte. Therefore I had no difficulty following the events on the ground and at sea. Even today I remember and can name all the rivers flowing into the Vistula river, the peninsulas of Europe starting from Kanin and Kola and on down and all the narrows and all the islands. I learned them in grade school geography.

I think young American readers who may be largely unacquainted with the sequence of events from Hitler's rise to power in 1933 will benefit from my brief outline. I feel compelled to add that your American grandfathers and grandmothers seemed little affected by the events of Europe in those days. They were preoccupied with the Great Depression at home and were often more interested in sports news which characteristically occupied (and still does) our newspapers' front pages.

Hitler and the Nazi party ascension to power on January 30th, 1933 sent shivers through the Jewish population in Germany and Poland. From day one Hitler had made no secret of his racist plans to eliminate Jews from life in Germany. In every raging speech he repeatedly blamed the Jews for all the ills of the world especially in Germany. Later in his book *Mein Kampf* he would sketch out plans for renouncing the Versailles Treaty which limited Germany's offensive potential and forced them to relinquish territories. He dreamed of building a thousand-year Reich and of restoring Germany's pride and power following their defeat in WWI which he blamed on the Jews. He promised that should international Jewry succeed in forcing another war on the world it would not end with the defeat of Germany but with the annihilation of the Jews.

As soon as he became Chancellor he moved to eliminate those Nazi Party leaders who were a potential threat to his dictatorial powers. During the action known as the "Night of Long Knives" he and his closest henchman, Heinrich Himmler, using Gestapo and SS gangs summarily executed hundreds of his potential opponents including most notably Roehm, the head of the powerful paramilitary SA and Strasser, the chief Nazi theoretician. He then turned to eliminating his potential opponents in the military and had the military swear allegiance to him only as "Der Fuehrer." All political parties except the Nazi party were abolished and forbidden and their leaders and prominent members were thrown into the concentration camps. He appointed Himmler head of the SS, the Gestapo and all police organizations and assumed the powers to rule by decree. Concentration camps, unknown before, were set up for jailing all political opponents, leaders of the parties, writers and intellectuals not towing the party line and Jews. The speed with which he was able to do this and gain the acquiescence of the majority of Germans was astounding. Of course as part of promised economic growth he started re-arming which pleased the military and steel magnates – the Krupps, Thyssens, Fricks and others – and which gave people jobs. Once again German citizens could visit their favorite bars and drink their beers in *Gemuetlichkeit* 'relaxation.' What was happening to Jews and to others not fortunate enough to be considered "pure" Aryan German citizens or the dismantling of all democratic institutions was not relevant to the majority.

In 1935 at the Nuernberg Gathering of the Party, Hitler announced the passage of racial laws defining exactly what constituted Jewish, half Jewish, one-quarter Jewish and so on. Jews were removed from all civil service positions and their businesses were either confiscated outright or they were forced to relinquish them to Germans for pennies on the dollar. A variety of other restrictions were enacted that effectively deprived them of any way to make a living. The noose around Jewish necks kept tightening more and soon even Jews who had welcomed the Nazis, preferring them to socialists or communists, could see no future for themselves in this land where they had lived for centuries and fought loyally in German wars.

Acts against the Jews culminated in 1938 with *Krystal Nacht* 'Night of Broken Glass' during which organized raids on Jewish businesses and homes were conducted. Windows were smashed, Jews were beaten or killed and many were sent to concentration camps. Jewish houses of worship were burned and hundreds of books by Jewish authors or opponents to Nazism were burned in bonfires. Jewish writer and poet Heinrich Heine's prophetic words, "If you start to burn books, you will soon burn people," would become all too true with the Holocaust.

Seeing no hope of moderating these policies Jews began looking for havens in other countries any which might accept them. Unfortunately most of the world gates were closed. Some renowned scientists and future Nobel Prize winners of their adopted countries found haven at universities in countries as far away as China. The rest had difficulties emigrating. The British sharply limited immigration to Palestine and issued a so-called "White Paper" renouncing the Balfour Declaration which had promised a new Jewish homeland in the ancient Jewish homeland won from the Ottoman Empire. Polish Jewish citizens living in Germany were simply rounded up and dumped on the Polish border.

About 350,000 German Jews eventually managed to escape and approximately 150,000 remained because they could find no haven anywhere or could not pay the exorbitant emigration fees assessed by the Nazis. Some hoped to "wait it out," banking on their hundreds of years of roots in Germany and the fact that they were veterans of German wars. Little did they dream that their war decorations or injuries would draw nothing but ridicule from the Nazis. That Germans, their *Landsleute* 'countrymen,' could become their killers never occurred to them. On the international scene, Hitler renounced the Versailles treaty and left the League of Nations. German troops marched into the "Rheinland" in violation of the Versailles agreement, then into Austria and finally into Czechoslovakia. Every step of the way Germany seemed to be appeased by England and France as well as other allies. In a sense it was understandable. In the aftermath of World War I, the war that was supposed to end all wars, memories of the horror were sharpened by works of such writers as Erich M. Remarque who described as well as anyone could the indescribable destruction. Clearly no one (other than Hitler) was in a mood to enter another war barely twenty years later. Sadly world tolerance of Germany's actions was later to extract a huge price – not only from Jews but also of so many others who were subdued by the Germans and even the Germans themselves. In defiance of Versailles Hitler had also built the most powerful army, navy and air force in the world. The world powers did not react with much more than with weak protests.

As a matter of fact, Hungary and Poland – the latter already a planned next victim – assisted him in the dismemberment of Czechoslovakia by demanding relinquishment of some territories. I remember the editorials in the Yiddish newspapers warning Poland of Hitler's intentions, pointing out that Hitler was not going to stop there - that his aim was to move further East to grab Wolhynia (Western Ukraine) with its fertile black soil and to move closer to the oil regions of Ploesti (Romania). This was his plan for expansion of his *Lebensraum* 'living space' the editorials warned. The Polish Government organized marches against the *Tschechs* and the people yelled *"Na Pepikow!"*[16]

Thus Czechoslovakia the only western style democracy in Eastern Europe was forced to give up Lower Silesia to Poland and Easter Slovakia to Hungary. To German people who may have still been skeptical of his dictatorial powers, Hitler proved that he could win without firing a single shot. And no sacrifices were required. They continued to indulge in the bounty he robbed from the Jews and the occupied territories. He seemed indeed to be the great genius that Providence had sent to Germany according to his henchman Himmler. Even the shrewd dictator Stalin miscalculated. Hitler, wanting to make sure that Stalin would not be in the way when he attacked Poland in 1939, signed a secret agreement with his archenemy whereby he let Stalin have half of Poland. Stalin thought that he was getting something for nothing. This giant blunder would later cost the Soviets the almost complete destruction of their land and cities and approximately 30 million dead. Of course to a tyrant like Stalin 30 million was just a number; he himself was responsible for the death of millions of his own people.

We in Poland viewed those developments and the concomitant increase of anti-Semitism in Poland with extreme anxiety. Uncle Joseph and my father began discussing emigration. One option was to have Joseph go to New York for the World's Fair and scan the opportunities there. As I remember it they thought also of Mexico and Palestine. My father argued against emigration pointing out that in Krosno we were considered well to

---

[16] 'Go after the *Tschechs.*'

do whereas in America even if we sold everything we would be paupers. Some people had made the choice to immigrate illegally. This would have never been an option for us. Nowadays immigrants complain about having to register each year. When I finally did come here in 1950, I duly registered every January, as did every immigrant I knew, and we had no complaints. We were thankful for being allowed to stay.

I believe that my parents' thoughts of emigration may have had more to do with the increasing anti-Semitism than with the threat of war although the latter may have also been a factor. As a teenager I was not greatly concerned about it. I actually thought it would be fun. I had rarely ventured even as far out of town as Jaslo, only about 15 miles away. If we moved to Palestine I could eat oranges and dates galore instead of the potatoes that were our main fare. My father, however, didn't think that a war would last more than days or weeks. After all he argued we now have poison gas and planes. And of course the World War I allies would intervene and Hitler would be forced to fight a two-front war.

When Poland started celebrating the crushing defeat of the 1409 German Teutonic (crusader) army under von Jungingen at the battle of Grunwald,[17] an historical event that had never been celebrated before, I sensed that something was in the air. The Polish-German relationship must have soured. Whereas during the *Tschech* crisis Poland and Germany were chummy; all of a sudden things had changed. Rumor had it that Hitler wanted Poland to relinquish a corridor through northern Poland to

---

[17] The Germans call it the battle at Tannenberg.

East Prussia. Nazis started anti-Polish activities in Danzig (Gdansk) claiming that Gdansk belonged to Germany.

Poland started preparing for possible war. At the *Przemyslowka*, 'evening school' I attended; we started to train using gas masks – in a gas chamber. People were learning to prepare make shift masks out of gauze. I became an air raid warden on our street. In case of an attack I was to rush people to designated cellars. For the first time I saw some two-engine airplanes at our Airbase in Krosno.

England and France hastily signed a non-aggression treaty with Poland in 1939 obligating them to come to Poland's assistance in case of German aggression. We trusted that this would keep Hitler away. From Italy the dictator Mussolini stuck his nose into the fray and offered to negotiate. Hitler outfoxed all of them by sending his Foreign Secretary von Ribentrop to Moscow to sign the agreement with Stalin. And he had his date for the attack on Poland set long beforehand for September 1, 1939. He started off with provocations, using prisoners from the concentration camp of Gross-Rosen in Germany dressed in Polish military uniforms supposedly attacking German border guards. He showed photos of the dead "Polish soldiers." British Prime Minister Neville Chamberlain who had visited Hitler during the *Tschech* crisis and had allegedly, "with Herr Hitler saved the peace," was trying to save it again.

Poland however was not going to give in under any pressure. Initially a partial, then a full mobilization was announced. The cities were darkened - windows were taped over to prevent splintering in case of bombing. People began hoarding food. The mood of Poland's citizens grew subdued. War was inevitable.

44

A group of young people from Krosno on a ski outing. The second from the right is my cousin David Fruhman who died in the gas chambers of Auschwitz together with his 5-year old son Michael and my 12-year old brother Henek. My cousin's wife had been shot in 1942. The girl in the center is my cousin Malka, shot in 1942, given away to the Gestapo by a Polish woman who was hiding her. A returning Polish soldier who had been dating her before the war sought her out and shot her.

The Jewish Gideon Club in Krosno. My two cousins were in this club as was the future wife of my cousin David. Both my cousins, David and Malka, as well as David's wife and son Michael didn't survive. Of the others, a few survived in Siberia.

45

This is a photo of the Betar (Zionist) organization - today's Likud. Some members of this Krosno group were in their brown uniforms when this photo was taken some time in the 1930's.

Another photo of my sister Mania (on the left, top row) and her friends. My cousin Ryvkah Platner is the fourth from the left in the front row. Most of them did not survive.

PART 3

The Invasion of Poland

(1939)

Primary public (Christian) school in Krosno: Teacher Mrs. Niedzielska with her pupils. Among them is fourteen year old Mania Bialywlos (arrow), my sister together with three other Jewish girls. - 1936

The Invasion of Poland (1939)

Around four o'clock on the morning of September 1, 1939 in the Polish town of Krosno just a few weeks after my sixteenth birthday I was awakened by the exploding sounds made by German '*Stukas*' or dive-bombers and the high-pitched blaring of the sirens that followed. Hitler's armies were invading Poland.

As an appointed warden of my street trained to use a gas mask at school I ran outside to urge people into the cellars designated as makeshift bomb shelters. Instead, we stood in the street watching the end of the precision bombing of our airport. Our homes sustained little damage while the oil refinery in Jedlicze near Krosno and the electricity plant in nearby Mecinka were bombed. The Stukas returned later in the day but they did not bomb the airbase again. Later we saw the battered wing of a German plane emblazoned with cross and swastika as it was being hauled along the main road of the town.

Although we in Krosno were aware of Germany's military preparations as the winds of war swept through Poland, the sudden blitz attack came as a shock.

In the days following, chaos reigned. Hitler's highly mechanized armies rapidly overran the relatively poor, rural country of Poland. The Polish army – including Polish Jews among the enlisted men and officers – was disorganized and still unprepared for mobilization. Stunned and confused, people gathered around the blaring radio outside the only electronic store in town. Adding to the confusion, most of the reports con-

tained all kinds of military code: "Attention!" Attention!" *'Nadchodzi'* –
codes which I assumed were warnings of oncoming planes. It was difficult to discern whether or where there was a frontline. New rumors spread
daily of the Allies, France and England fulfilling their obligation according to their non-aggression treaty with Poland and coming at last to Pol-
and's assistance.

At the beginning people thought that this war, unlike World War I,
would not last more than a few days. After all, in contrast to World War I,
we now had planes, tanks and poison gas. What's more, people assumed
that the British and French would attack from the West and face Hitler
with a two-front war. Bismarck had said that Germany must at all cost
avoid a two-front war that could not be won. It was not to be.

The Allies, instead of attacking while Hitler was preoccupied with
Poland, sat idly in their fortifications including the supposedly impenetra-
ble Maginot Line. They did not seem to grasp the reality of the war until
1940 when Hitler transferred the bulk of his army from Poland to the West
and began an aggressive attack.

In a few days rumors began to spread that German troops were advancing rapidly toward the Vistula River, the river in Poland that origi-
nated in the Carpathian Mountains in the south and flowed into the Baltic
Sea to the north. The Polish army's only remaining hope was to create a
line of defense along the river. The Polish Government had already eva-
cuated Warsaw and moved – or rather escaped – to southeast Poland, near
the Romanian border.

People at last started responding to the situation. The Orthodox
Jews cut their beards and replaced their *caftans* with jackets, pants and

caps. Jews stopped attending services at the synagogue and instead prayed at home or assembled at someone's home in the neighborhood.[18] Everywhere preparations for evacuation were under way.

Unaware of Hitler's secret pact with Stalin to divide Poland, the eastern half of the country going to Stalin, many people began fleeing eastward. My uncle Joseph Platner, my mother's brother and our partner in the glass business just managed to get himself and his family onto the eastbound train out of Krosno.

At our house we had lengthy ongoing discussions about what to do next but we seemed paralyzed. By the time my father and our family finally decided to get moving my Uncle Platner's chosen route of escape – the trains – was no longer open. A bombing raid destroyed the train station while we were on the way there. In shock, we returned home.

The world seemed to be turning upside down yet many did nothing.

My Uncle Chaim Fruhman and his wife Sarah, my mother's sister, refused to leave and instead decided to move into our house in the center of town where it was thought they would be safer. Uncle Abraham Platner, my mother's brother and his wife Hencia and their son Aaron and daughters Sarah and Rachel also decided to stay in Krosno as did Uncle Mordechai, my mother's oldest brother and his wife Chana and their daughters Beila and Doba.

What were they thinking?

---

[18] According to Jewish law certain prayers may only be said in the presence of a *minyan*, ten adult male Jews.

"I am not afraid of the Germans," Uncle Chaim often said. "What can they do to me?" "Marinate me?" "Put me to work?" "I have worked all my life anyway." He spoke from his experience in World War I when the Axis troops of the Austro-Hungarian Empire behaved humanely and actually called on the support of Jews then escaping from Czarist troops to Austria and Germany.

Uncle Chaim didn't realize that he was dealing with another Germany altogether, a Germany transformed by Hitler and his SS robots. His blind trust eventually cost him and most of his family their lives.

I had three first cousins named Joseph and we nicknamed each according to his hair color. The redhead, a Platner, was Red Joe. The light blond – whose father, Uncle Abraham had decided not to flee – was White Joe – also a Platner. The brunette was Black Joe, a Fruhman. My Platner cousins Red Joe and White Joe and Red Joe's sister Genia left on foot eastward in the company of Uncle Chaim's eight sons and daughters. My father gave each one of them a twenty dollar gold coin to take on the road.

With the train station destroyed my father called on a Polish peasant from a nearby village of Kroscienko to take us eastward. Joseph Socha used to work for us transporting glass in his horse-drawn wagon from our wholesale warehouse at the railroad station to the surrounding communities. We had no particular idea where we would go but just away from the oncoming German armies. We packed a few items in pillowcases, loaded them on his horse-drawn cart and went on northeastward toward the town of Przemysl on the San River.

The German army was rumored to be advancing rapidly across the Vistula River. Hoping against hope, we still imagined that the Vistula

52

River might stop the Germans. When this happened, we fantasized, we would be able to return home.

The going was difficult as the roads were clogged with military and refugee traffic and continually strafed by German Stukas. It was stop and go, frequently stopping and running in terror into the woods by the roadside as the Stukas appeared and showered us with machine-gun fire.

We finally made it to the small town of Dynow before Przemysl. Here my father decided not to go any further. We were accommodated with other refugees in the small house of the President of the Jewish community. We slept on the floor. The entire house was filled with refugees; our clothing crumpled into pillows under our heads. To us kids who had rarely ventured out of town it was at times more like an adventure, an outing, or bivouac. My parents, however, lamented the loss of their own beds.

"Oy!" "My bed" my father complained. To this day whenever I plop into my bed after a full day on my feet, my joints aching, I feel the same way, "Oy!" "My bed."

A few days later a unit of German infantry quietly appeared at the Market Square in town. They set up their field-kitchen and appeared rather friendly, distributing candy to the kids. I myself didn't approach them for fear of being pointed out by the Gentile kids as Jewish but watched them from a short distance. Since it appeared quiet my father and a few other refugees decided to return home. My father planned to get as far as Korczyna a small town only five kilometers from Krosno and leave us for the time being in Dynow. There he would get information as to the situation in Krosno and if it was safe he would send for us.

He could not know that the very next day all hell would break loose in Dynow.

A unit of *Schwarzhemden*, black-uniformed SS men, entered the town while the military unit moved eastward. In the early afternoon a giant commotion was heard outside the straw-roofed little house of a local glazier we had known and were now staying with. Loud speakers ordered all male Jews between sixteen and sixty to report to the Central Market Square. We heard screaming and crying. I was frightened. My mother seated us at the kitchen table and gave each one of us a book to read as if we were busy reading and hadn't noticed what was going on outside. Our host, an elderly glazier, ran down to the basement to hide. He put on some of his deceased wife's clothes and a babushka over his head as a woman. Another boy my age and his mother stayed in the next room.

Just then an SS man in his black uniform including a black helmet with a swastika kicked open the door of the kitchen with his boot.

"ALL MEN OUT!" He yelled in German aiming his revolver at us. My heart must have pounded in my chest and the adrenalin must have been flowing madly in my veins but I remember only the exchange of words that followed.

"What about him?," My mother asked with an absolute calm that belied what she must have felt.

"How old is he?," the SS man inquired.

"He's only fourteen," my mother answered although I was actually sixteen.

"He can stay," came the response.

My mother's knowledge of German acquired when she attended a German School during the Austrian rule of our town by King Franz Joseph may have saved my life.

The SS man shoved the Hebrew books off the table and entered the next room. He ordered the boy there out to the assembly point in the market square. Then he left.

Later that afternoon we again heard chaos and screaming outside. Peering cautiously through our window we saw a huge fireball torching the old gothic-style Jewish temple near the square. We heard the following day that the SS had ordered some elderly Orthodox Jews into the temple to remove the parchment scrolls inscribed with the words of the Torah or Hebrew bible. Once the Jews were inside the SS men locked the doors to the temple, poured gasoline along the perimeter and then burned the Jews alive together with the sacred texts.

That night we did not sleep.

Very early the following morning my mother answered a soft knocking at the door. There stood the sixteen-year-old who had been sent out the day before to the market square. My mother let him in. He appeared very pale and bloodied as he sat down and began to spill out the following story.

The SS man ordered the Jews assembled at the square to line up. About a dozen of them were taken away and the teen and the rest of the group were marched down to a wooded area at the edge of town. Here the Nazis ordered them to stand alongside a ravine and then machine-gunned them to death. As the sound of the machine guns began blasting the air the boy fainted and dropped to the ground with the dead piling up on him.

When he awoke the killers were gone. He worked himself out from under the mass of the dead and made his way back to the place we were staying.

About a half an hour later a man from Krosno, Mr. Schamroth, appeared at our door. We knew him as the owner of a bike store in Krosno as we had often rented bikes from him. He had a bullet wound in his chest and described the same events. The lucky dozen who had escaped this fate were taken to the SS quarters where they were beaten and forced to clean the floors and latrines. We learned this from one of the lucky ones, Srulek Palant, of Krosno. This was our first exposure – but not our last – to SS inhumanity. Not in our wildest dreams could be have imagined such mass murder of innocent humans.[19]

During those early massacres, women, elderly and children were spared. Beginning in 1942 they would be the first to perish while the young and healthy would be spared – at least for a while – so they could perform the slave labor needed to grease the vast machinery of Hitler's war.

Much worse by far was still to come.

On that very day Mr. Socha brought us a note from my father describing his ordeal on the way home to Korczyna. He must have been quite shaken by his encounter with the Germans enroute for in the note he quoted from the *Yom Kippur*, the Day of Atonement liturgy, "There are

---

[19] We had heard of civil rights abuses in Germany since Hitler came to power; concentration camps, the burning of Jewish houses of worship, the confiscation of property, maltreatment and even some killings but mass murder on such a scale and in a respected civilized society was incomprehensible. Equally disturbing was the indifference of the general population and indeed the world to what was happening. This apathy and acquiescence to Hitler's policies by most Germans paved the way for the murder that we were experiencing now.

those that pay with their money and those who pay with their lives." As my father was making his way to Korczyna the Nazis stopped him and confiscated all his money. This time he paid with his money but next time, he seemed to feel, he might pay with his life.

In Krosno and the vicinity my father reported that everything was quiet but extremely tense and regimented by the Nazi occupiers who did not hesitate to evict people from their homes and who forced able bodied citizens to clean streets and latrines and to restore the bombed airbase.

My father urged us to return home but to avoid main roads. Accompanied by Srulek Palant who had survived the Dynow massacre we rode home as we had left it in Mr. Socha's wagon. Just as we arrived and were getting down from the wagon we learned of an order issued by the Gestapo for Jews to leave the town and evacuate to the east side of the San River, the future demarcation line agreed to by Stalin and Hitler.

Srulek Palant got back on the wagon. My family and I were about to do the same but suddenly the course of our lives was changed – as it would again later for a second time – by the arrival of a Gestapo man named Becker. Becker stopped us and ordered my father not to leave.

"You are needed here," Becker said.

Because we had the only window-glass establishment in town the German occupiers considered us essential to the town and the German war economy. We watched as what might be our last chance of survival disappeared with a creaking of the wheels of Socha's wagon which would take Srulek Palant and a few others the 40 kilometers to Sanok and across the San River into the hands of the Soviets. Before the war was over these compatriots would be condemned to Siberia.

Who could possibly know which fate would mean survival and which would mean death? Yet Siberia, a place at the end of the earth, meant survival for some in my family compared to the death awaiting those who remained in German-occupied Poland. Srulek Palant was to be lucky again even in Siberia and despite all the odds.

The German forces withdrew to the previously agreed line of demarcation in Poland, essentially the old so-called Curzon line running along the San and Bug rivers. The German part of Poland became the "General Government" under the Nazi Governor Attorney and past court defender of Hitler, Hans Frank.

What happened to my cousins? Uncle Joseph and his family as well as the Fruhman cousins managed to get as far as Stanislawow in Poland now Ukraine. Against the urgings of their Fruhman cousins to continue eastward with them White Joe and Red Joe stopped in German occupied Ustrzyki to say the Sabbath prayers.[20] This act of piety sent them to their final rest for as they were searching for a place where Sabbath service might be held they were shot and killed by a *Sonderkommando* special command of SS like the one that massacred the Jews of Dynow.[21]

Later on an exchange with the Soviets allowed western refugees in the Soviet zone to return to their homes in the German zone of occupation.

---

[20] The Sabbath was a day of rest and they did not wish to violate it by continuing to walk.

[21] The Gestapo in Krosno later allowed us to go to Ustrzyki Dolne to open their graves and bury their bodies in our own Jewish cemetery in Krosno provided their families signed a document testifying that they died during the air raid. The boys' fathers, my uncles Abraham and Mordechai, signed and both cousins were brought to Krosno and buried in our cemetery there. The crying of their mothers Hencia and Chana was ceaseless.

This was meant mainly for ethnic Germans and Poles, nevertheless most Jewish refugees registered for the exchange, preferring even the harshest circumstances under the Germans – as long as the killing had stopped – to living in a strange city under the Soviets.

As the Jews registered for transfer the Soviet secret service picked them up and deported them to Siberia. Among them were my Uncle Joseph Platner and his family, some of the Fruhman cousins, Srulek Palant and other refugees from Krosno who eventually survived the war in Siberia[22]. The few cousins who managed to escape deportation to Siberia and later slipped back into Krosno eventually died in the Holocaust.

The Formation of Judenrats (1940)

In Krosno as in other towns of the General Government the Gestapo now assumed complete charge of the Jews and ordered the formation of the *Judenrats,* councils of Jewish elders, responsible for providing a Jewish workforce for menial labor and carrying out other tasks ordered by the Gestapo. The Gestapo selected Judah Engel, a German Jew and native of Krosno, to form the *Judenrat* in our town. In 1938 Engel was one of many Polish-born Jews like Herschel Gruenspans' father, deported from Germany and dumped by the Nazis on the Polish border. As the new leader of our Jewish council Mr. Engel selected my father to serve as a member of the group – a mixed blessing at best but one he had no choice but to receive.

---

[22] For more information on the Siberian story, please read *Surviving the Holocaust in Siberia – the Diary of Pearl Minz.*

Jewish businesses and homes were confiscated. The Germans appointed a new mayor, an ethnic German, to replace Mr. Bergman the owner of a brick factory who along with his brother, a baker, and a number of other Polish patriots, politicians and intellectuals had been taken away by the Gestapo never to be heard from again.[23] The new mayor opened a *Kaffee Haus*, a coffee house, frequented mostly by Germans and he kept us busy making beveled glass plates for the tables, glass cabinets for pastries and by framing pictures. As long as the blatant mass murders stopped – and they did in 1939 and 1940 – we were glad to be in our own town. Work didn't bother us. We were used to it. Somehow we managed to go on with our lives in spite of tremendous hardships and deprivations. German soldiers would frequently tip us with a few German marks and more often with a loaf or two of bread or canned goods.

Food was rationed – a portion to non-Jewish Poles, a much smaller portion to Jews. In my family we wore the Star of David armbands and observed the other restrictions placed on all Jews at that time but as skilled craftsmen in a business important to the war economy we were somewhat more respected and better off than the other Jews.

My family's glass business was confiscated and a *Treuhander*, a trustee, appointed to administer it. It was a fully stocked wholesale glass warehouse located at the railroad station with its own rail-side. Most of the glass was shipped to Germany.[24] Our glazing, framing and glass-beveling workshop in town was left entirely to us. We worked steadily for

---

[23] They were presumably executed.

[24] Later my father was called to the Gestapo and asked to give an estimate of the quantity and approximate value of the stored glass. The trustee was arrested for allegedly taking bribes and profiteering from the sale of glass on the black market.

the Germans especially the military glazing broken windows in their vehicles and their quarters, framing pictures of Hitler, certificates of promotion and family photographs. Eventually an ethnic German became our
Treuhander and we were essentially his employees but he gave us full
freedom to do as we liked while he served as a translator for the *Ortsko-
mandantur,* the German regional military command.

German work kept us busy and the other Jewish craftsmen and
shopkeepers as well, especially the electro-mechanic Mr. Schachner, the
tailors Goebel and Berger, the shoemakers and others. Schachner's shop
was particularly busy with German vehicles both military and SS waiting
to have the electrical systems repaired. Bumping along Polish dirt roads,
the German vehicles often cracked a windshield and this kept us busy with
making repairs.

Early in 1940 Jews were ordered to prepare for evacuation to the
East. We were told to assemble blankets and three days worth of provisions should the order be issued for resettlement. A time was not given.
After a while, as nothing came of it, we relaxed hoping that they had
changed their minds. Life went on.

In the city administration there was a German whom the Jews
nicknamed the *Schwitzer* meaning "sweating" because he always seemed
to be in a rush. He was a rather benign character, very polite, bowing and
greeting even as he entered a Jewish store. Of course neither he nor the

Civil Administration made any decisions regarding the Jews. This was the exclusive province of the Gestapo, the arbiters of life and death.[25]

One day a '*Deutsches Geschaeft,*' an exclusive store strictly for Germans opened up across the street from our shop. It was managed by a former Polish Air Force officer from the Krosno Airbase, a certain Mr. Peck who had now registered as an ethnic German with all its accrued privileges. The store was expanded to include store space in the building of Mr. Moses and in an adjacent building owned by my father and my uncle Joseph Platner.

Of course Jews no longer owned property of any kind. All Jewish properties were confiscated so no permission was required from either Mr. Moses or from my family. The goods that stocked this German store were available only to Germans.

"Jews and dogs forbidden"

Read a large sign, hanging on the door. Some Poles declared themselves ethnic Germans or '*Volksdeutsch*' so they could participate in the wholesale confiscation of Jewish stores and homes. One such was the Lewandowski family. Mr. Lewandowski once worked in a rubber factory owned by two Jews from the city of Tarnow. Their teenage daughter Halina shopped for the family in the German store and often slipped surreptitiously into our shop to sell us provisions of all sorts difficult to obtain otherwise.

---

[25] At the end of the war the Gestapo chief in Krosno, a man named Schmatzler, and Schwitzer were caught trying to escape from the city. In their trial Schwitzer was released and Schmatzler was sentenced to death and executed.

The black market in German marks thrived just as the post-war American script would later. German soldiers coming to our shop often exchanged German marks for Polish *zlotys* doubling and sometimes even tripling the profit I made by selling the marks to a Jewish dealer. We survived. It was much more difficult for others who didn't have such contacts. Assigned menial jobs, they had difficulty feeding their families especially in winter. We still lived in the same place but Jews in more comfortable accommodations had to give them up to the German occupiers and move to humbler quarters. Jews who were not craftsmen got jobs building roads or clearing them of snow, house cleaning for the German military and other menial jobs.

The Germans and Soviets were still chummy in 1939 and 1940 so we received occasional mail or messages from Uncle Joseph and our cousins trapped on the Soviet side. Most were anxious to return home even with the hardships and harassments of the anti-Semitic laws and the mandatory Star of David armbands. My cousins Moniek and Hanka Fruhman registered for the legitimate exchange to return to Krosno as did Uncle Joseph Platner and his family but they were considered by the Soviets as *'unreliables'* and were deported to Siberia.

The Gestapo Headquarters known in Krosno as *Sicherheitsamt*[26] *Jaslo, Grenzpolizeikommisariat Krosno*, were located across from our shop on Ordynacka Street. Mr. Schachner's electrical shop was just around the corner. The head of the Krosno Gestapo was a short fat ruddy-faced man named *Hauptsturmfuehrer Schmatzler*. His deputy was *Obers-*

---

[26] Security office

turmfuehrer von Davier. Others whose names I recall are *Untersturm-fuehrer Stengler* or *Stentzler* and *Sturmman* Becker and a Gestapo man named Hauch. *Sturmman* Becker spoke a broken Polish and probably was a *Volksdeutsche* from somewhere in western Poland. He was responsible for a number of shooting sprees of Jews in Krosno.

The Chief of the Jaslo Headquarters was *Hauptsturmfuehrer* von Raschwitz. Since we were across the street we often observed their comings and goings. When they came into our shop they behaved like any normal customer. I remember framing *Schmatzler's* promotion diploma with the final sentence *"Sie koennen sich dem Schutze des Fuehrer's sicher sein,"* 'You can be assured of the Fuehrer's protection.' The Chief of the Gestapo for the entire General Government was *Sturmbannfuehrer* Krueger, a Himmler protégé.

In 1939 and 1940 sporadic shootings occurred for transgressions such as not wearing the armband. On one occasion when two Jews were killed the *Ortskommandant* or German regional military commander called for Mr. Engel of the *Judenrat* for information on the shooting. The *Ortskommandant*, a colonel, expressed his sorrow and offered condolences to the families of the victims. He had no authority over SS actions.

"We are all not like that," he said – a remarkable statement from a German colonel.

In general the Jews working for the military were rarely mistreated.

The frequency of such episodes increased as time passed but for the time being there were no more massacres.

My father was an Orthodox Jew and we kept a kosher home but it quickly became impossible to keep kosher. Any food you could scavenge was needed for survival. Once a German soldier offered my father and me a bowl of soup with pork in it. It was the first time I tasted pork and the smell of it nauseated me. I didn't want to insult the officer so I ate it but I kept holding my breath so I couldn't taste it. Later in the concentration camp a piece of speck or bacon was a delicacy.

Schools closed and school buildings became the offices of the German military. People tried to lead as normal a life as possible and when they could afford it, they hired a private teacher to teach their children at home. Religious services ceased but people got together in private homes and conducted brief Sabbath and holiday services and even baked matzah for Passover. Living in a small town where people knew one another made survival easier than in the large ghettos in Warsaw and elsewhere. But we still experienced shortages of various kinds. Oils and fats for example were hard to get.[27] One day Moshe Heller and I were glazing a window at a gymnasium that housed the German military. A drunken soldier ordered me to dispose of his washbasin. When I had the chutzpah to tell him that I wasn't there for that purpose he slapped me and accused me of being the one to smear a Star of David on the glass panes in another window – a thing I would not have dared doing. He threatened to call the Gestapo.

---

[27] A miner once brought us paraffin oil from the oil wells in our area, supposedly for cooking. My mother tried to fry potato pancakes with it but it tasted and smelled of pure naphtha.

Moshe apologized to the soldier and ordered me to empty the bucket which I did. The other soldiers in the room held the guy back and told me to disappear. This is the only time I was physically mistreated by a German soldier until later on in the Concentration Camp of Krakow-Plaszow.[28]

Our synagogue became a stable and thus was spared destruction at the hands of the arsonists - the fate of many synagogues in Europe in these years. The original Jewish population of Krosno was about two or three thousand souls but it doubled as Jews were forcibly relocated in Krosno from areas newly annexed to Germany such as the *Warthegau* and especially *Lodz, Litzmanstadt*. Later on the Jews of Krosno had to accommodate Jews expelled from their homes in the villages and small towns in the outlying areas – a situation which caused tremendous crowding.

In 1940 the German armies went into the offensive in the West. They overran Belgium and Holland, maneuvered around the Maginot Line and within five weeks occupied all of France. They invaded Denmark and Norway and routed an English force which managed to land in Narvik in northern Norway. Hitler stopped the offensive only when he had encircled the Allies at Dunkirk – a blunder that allowed Churchill to transfer a large portion of the Expeditionary Force and many French forces to England.

Hitler was winning on all fronts – at sea and on land. Soon his forces occupied nearly all of Europe. We Jews became very pessimistic as we overheard the daily reports from the German military command broadcasting via the radio their Navy successes under Admiral Raeder and later

---

[28] The concept of 'mistreatment,' however, does not begin to capture the deep trauma I experienced as a hostage of and witness to the German atrocities of these years.

Doenitz and their rapid progress on all fronts including Denmark, Norway and later, the Balkans. The German Africa Corps under General Rommel took over from the beleaguered Italians in North Africa and fought the Eighth British Army under different commanders including General Montgomery.

The Germans seemed invincible.

Admiration for the Fuehrer reached a high point. He became in the eyes of ordinary Germans the greatest military genius of all time. Thanks to the Fuehrer they now ruled nearly all Europe and the Jews, the *Untermenschen* 'sub-humans,' one step below the Slavs – were at last deprived of their freedom and their rights.

But we were still alive and still for the most part living in our own homes.

The Eastern Offensive (1941)

1939 ended and 1940 passed by with the Germans at the zenith of their power. Then came 1941. Relations between Hitler and Stalin soured. All of a sudden we noticed heavy German military traffic moving eastward especially at night. Our sleep was disturbed by the rumbling of tanks along the roads that had only recently been turned from dirt to cobblestone by Jewish forced labor. Day and night the transports rolled. Railroad traffic increased dramatically. Building activity of all sorts including the building of barracks and roads also increased. Air traffic at the airbase in Krosno was very busy.

Something was brewing.

Suddenly graffiti such as *"Der russischer Schwein verlangt was ist nicht sein"*[29] appeared on the trucks and trains.

Living in our building was a German SA by the name of Mr. Paes whose radio now blared intense anti-Soviet propaganda from his window into our courtyard. Even more unnerving was the constant stream of anti-Semitic propaganda. For years now we had been forced to listen to these hate messages about the war mongering Jews of London and Washington but now new tirades were added, this time against the Jews of Moscow – thus creating a triumvirate of evil that the "peace-loving" Hitler was forced to fight in order to save Western Civilization.

Germans like Mr. Paes seemed to eat it up. Why shouldn't they? After their defeat and degradation of World War I, they were now the Lords of Europe. Hitler was their redeemer, their Messiah. The hearts of many Germans seemed to hold the fervent wish that, "The Fuehrer knows what he is doing and the *Endsieg* – the 'final victory' – will be ours."

On June 22, 1941 in the early morning we were awakened by noisy air traffic. Soon Mr. Paes's radio was blaring martial music followed by the announcement of the Oberkommando der Wehrmacht:[30]

The German Armies in order to defend itself against
Soviet aggression was forced to cross the borders into
The Polish territory occupied by the Soviets. The bas-
tardly Jewish war-mongers in Moscow and London
have forced this war on the German people.

---

[29] "The Russian swine demands what is not his," a reference to the Soviets annexation of the Baltic States, Moldavia and Bukowina, a part of Romania.
[30] "The Supreme Command of the Army"

It reminded me of Hitler's announcements in 1939 at the start of the invasion of Poland *Es wird gegengeschosen*, 'We are shooting back,' – as if it were the Poles who started the attack on Germany and Hitler was just defending his country.

Mr. Paes, a native Berliner who belonged to the organization *Todt*, 'Pioneer units' was the head truck dispatcher in Krosno. His wife, an ugly woman if ever there was one reminded me of Quasimoto in the Hunchback of Notre Dame. A homosexual, he took a liking to me and "asked" my mother to allow me to stay overnight in his apartment "in case of an air raid."

My mother was frightened but she had no choice but to let me go. When I got there he started his tricks but I was non-responsive and he let me go. On another occasion he appeared with his face full of black and blue marks. When I asked what had happened he had told me that he had fallen off the stairs. His maid later told me the true story. He had given a private drinking party to which he invited two airmen from the Airbase. At the end of the party he tried his tricks with one of them. The airman had grabbed him by his genitals twisted him around and threw him down the stairs.

Only a few hours later after the announced outbreak of Operation Barbarossa, airmen coming to our shop described their bombing sorties of Soviet positions and their bombing raid on the airbase around Lemberg[31] in the dark early morning hours. They described how they saw people

---

[31] Lwow

running out of buildings in their underwear. The Germans had taken the Soviets completely by surprise.

Within days thousands of Soviet war prisoners were marched through our town into a prisoner of war camp hastily built in the nearby village of Szebnie. This camp later became a concentration camp for Poles and Jews but only after 5,000 Soviet prisoners of war were shot in a ravine near the camp.[32] The German armies moved quickly, repeating the Blitzkrieg tactics they had employed the year before in Poland and France. They encircled hundreds of thousands of Soviets and murdered many thousands of prisoners. Jewish prisoners of war and Soviet commissars fell under the SS's jurisdiction instead of the army's and the SS summarily executed them by the thousands.[33] Within weeks the German army forced the Soviets out of the Baltic States and surrounded Leningrad. The Germans also made rapid progress on the southern front. Operation Barbarossa – the code name for the attack on the Soviet Union – was in full swing.[34]

The Germans were for the most part welcomed by the native populations of the Baltic States, the Ukraine and Moldavia. With their innate hatred of the Soviets and communism, inhabitants of these regions saw the German occupiers as liberators. Hitler promised them freedom and inde-

---

[32] Today a memorial stands at the site of the massacre.

[33] Is it then any wonder that as the German fortunes changed the Soviets took horrible revenge?

[34] Little did its commanders know that Hitler's plan to finish the war by Christmas 1941 would go seriously awry as the German forces unprepared for the Russian frosts pushed deeper into the vast Soviet Union and winter started early.

pendence. But they later came to realize that they had simply exchanged one tyrant for another.[35]

Hitler and Himmler now took advantage of the anti-Semitic up-bringings and feelings of the people of this Eastern region. The Germans now used their *Sonderkommandos* with the help of the native Fascists to murder Jews by the hundreds of thousands. The native volunteers didn't need much persuasion to participate – because after all, "Didn't the International Jews force communism on them and persecute them?" It is well documented that Himmler's orders to his troops explicitly expressed his preference for using the native population and volunteers called *Hivis* or *Hilfswillige* for the dirty work of killing.[36] Post-war trial court records of perpetrators' testimony provide detailed information of the atrocities committed by the Special *Sonderkommandos* and their native assistant *Hivis*.[37]

The war crimes committed in 1939 pale in comparison to the massacres committed by the *Sonderkommandos* and the *Hivis* as the German forces marched into Soviet occupied territories. From time to time a Jew miraculously escaped one of these massacres and returned then to Krosno

---

[35] Hitler appointed Alfred Rosenberg, a high-ranking Nazi of Eastern origin, in charge of the Eastern territories, rather than giving them independence. Never a part of Hitler's overall plan for the "new order in Europe," they joined the Poles in becoming the wood-choppers and water carriers for the glorious German race.

[36] Himmler himself was concerned about the effects that the savagery of mass murder – of women and children no less – would have on the German soldiers when they returned to their own families.

[37] For those interested in a brief description of those tragedies I will refer to the booklet of Christopher Browning, Professor of History at the Pacific Lutheran University, which can be purchased for $12 and can be read over a weekend.

to speak of it. It was almost unbelievable but in the heart of each Jew in Krosno was the question, "Are we going to be next?"

The extermination camps and the gassing of millions were still to come.

Why shouldn't the Nazis proceed with their plans for the more effective mass killing when the Swedes were selling steel to them and the Swiss were still doing big business with them – when the world was silent about the atrocities and didn't seem to care about annihilation of the Jewish people? The United States was not yet at war but it is now an established fact that certain high government officials in the United States knew what was happening as did the Pope who was in contact with Catholic clergy in Poland, Berlin, Budapest and Bucharest. The silence of the world against the enormity of the crimes is difficult to comprehend.

Around mid-December 1941 the Gestapo in Krosno ordered the *Judenrat* to report to their office. As my father prepared to cross the street to the Gestapo office we became very frightened of what they had in store for us. I kept watch through our shop window and I saw my father with his back to the window across the street. After about half an hour – an eternity it seemed – my father returned and told us the following story.

The Gestapo assembled the *Judenrat* and demanded that within twenty-four hours the Jews of Krosno deliver all their furs and woolens, even the smallest pieces – everything – to a designated collection site. When Mr. Engel, the President of the *Judenrat* asked a question he was slapped in the face and told that any Jew caught with such materials would be shot on the spot. My father overheard an SS man from Jaslo telling

Schmatzler the Gestapo chief in Krosno, *"Knallen sie einige weg"* – 'Knock a few off.'

We collected all our woolens, even torn stockings and all furs or clothes with a piece of fur on them and delivered them the following morning as ordered. Becker shot a few Jews that day including Miss Furst in her little kiosk for allegedly hoarding a pair of fur gloves. Others were killed for alleged possession of a woolen sock – all part of the fear tactics that my father overheard discussed the evening before. The furs and woolens were shipped to Germany for the soldiers now contending with the Russian winter.

On the 7th of December 1941 President Roosevelt's "Day of Infamy," the Japanese suddenly and unexpectedly attacked Pearl Harbor and nearly destroyed the American Pacific fleet. The radio in Mr. Paes' apartment facing our courtyard was blaring with martial music as the news was being broadcast. The Germans were elated. They now had the Japanese as partners in the war.[38] A few days later as Hitler proudly declared war on the United States the Jews saw the inevitable American response as a ray of hope in an otherwise hopeless situation.

The Germans were stopped in their tracks on the Eastern Front as winter began but this news gave us little hope. By mid-December the German forces had surrounded Leningrad and reached the outskirts of Moscow.

---

[38] Little did they realize that they awakened a sleeping colossus who would eventually bring about their own destruction.

Killing on a New Scale (1942)

About this time, we heard rumors that in the city of Chelmno Jews were being loaded into airtight specially constructed vans and gassed. We were urged not to believe it and to avoid spreading rumors and chaos. The infamous extermination camps for Jews were not yet in full operation but Auschwitz was a burgeoning slave labor camp mainly for Polish political prisoners, Polish patriots and members of the Polish underground as well as anyone the Germans considered a saboteur.[39] Conducting systematic abductions in the Polish towns, the Germans grabbed Polish workers off the streets and shipped them to Germany for slave labor. The Germans also used Soviet war prisoners in Auschwitz for gassing experiments - initially with carbon monoxide from captured Soviet diesel tanks and later with cyanide gas.

In early February 1942 a man employed at the airbase in Krosno came to our shop and asked to speak to my father in private. He worked for a German concern *Chemische Werke Askania* of Berlin Charlottenburg and used to purchase glass from us and give glazing jobs to our firm. He told my father that he was a Jew from Oppeln, then in Germany, even though he wore no armband with the Star of David. He had information he said from a reliable German source that the SS planned to exterminate all Jews by the end of 1942.

He asked my father to find a hiding place and said that he would like to join us. When my father told us the story we just simply did not

---

[39] This included peasants who didn't deliver their assigned quotas of agricultural products or who hoarded food, incited against the Germans, secretly listened to foreign broadcasts or possessed radios or guns.

believe him. How is it possible to kill so many people especially since we were thought indispensible to the German war economy? Even the memory of the massacres of Jews in the Ghettos in the large cities – even with the presence of freshly constructed concentration camps such as Auschwitz – even with the evidence of the power and viciousness of Hitler's regime, it was difficult to believe.[40]

We wanted to deny that it was possible. How did we know that this man was Jewish and not a Nazi agent? Where would we hide? Which Pole would risk his own life and the lives of his family by hiding Jews? Would we even want to impose on them such risks? Hiding Jews was a dangerous affair and it took exceptional human beings to agree to it. Already Germans searched Polish homes for hidden Jews and for those hiding in the surrounding forests. We kept silent about this man's disclosure and went about our work as before but with new fear in our souls.

The murder and disappearance of Jews for spurious reasons was on the rise. Some of those who disappeared were probably taken to build the gassing camps. One day a glazier named Nathan Beim was jailed overnight in Krosno. Shortly afterward Gestapo Becker was seen leading Beim in chains to the train station. My brothers' classmate, a boy named Kern, who worked for the German Kirchoff Company building roads was injured on the job when he was caught between two trucks and broke several ribs. He was taken to the hospital. When Gestapo Becker learned of this he went to the hospital and shot the teenager in his bed.

---

[40] The Jew from Oppeln was of course right about our fate. His information probably came from someone aware of the Wannsee Conference in Berlin that outlined the extermination of the Jewish people.

By Gestapo order a few Jews had to standby every night in case a German needed help digging a truck out of the snow or for other chores deemed beneath the Master Race. The schedule of "volunteers" for this night duty was organized by the *Judenrat* but Gestapo Becker kept a few hostages there and sometimes he stopped by at night simply to shoot them at random. A boy named Sanale Rivalis – his mother's name was Riva, thus his nickname, which means 'belonging to Riva' – was shot by Becker in this manner as were others whose names I do not know.

When the situation appeared hopeless some handicapped people requested to be euthanized. Once my father was asked to serve as a kind of judge in such a case. A handicapped man with a university education in philosophy insisted on euthanasia and the man's family asked my father to judge whether according to Jewish law this was permissible. I remember how my father agonized about it. He spoke to the rabbi in town as well as to Dr. Rosenberg who was to perform the euthanasia. Finally he went to the man's house and discussed it with him. There were a few respected Jews there that the man wished to be present. Dr. Rosenberg injected him with a large dose of morphine and he died.

My father came home from this ordeal very depressed as were we.

In May 1942 the German spring offensive was in full swing on the Eastern Front. German forces again pushed deeper into the Soviet Union and eventually reached Stalingrad on the Volga River. The Crimea and the fortress of Sevastopol were in German hands. The situation as we saw it was hopeless despite the occasional good news such as the British defeat of Germany's Africa corps under General Rommel at Tobruk and El Alamein and General Patton's arrival in the European theater of war.

In May 1942 we received orders from the Gestapo to build a Ghetto in Krosno on a part of the *Franciszkanska* 'Franciscan' street starting near a property belonging to the Franciscan Church at the house of my uncle Joseph Platner – now in Siberia – and ending with the house of Mr. Dym, an area that included only four or five houses. We were to brick up the windows to the outside so that they opened only to the front of the street and to a small plaza that once was the neighborhood's egg and poultry market. A gate was constructed next to the Franciscan Church property and Jews were allowed to pass through the gate only with a permit from the Gestapo or as a part of a work detail. Everyone working in our shop had such a permit signed by Gestapo von Davier allowing us free movement in and out of the Ghetto. Two policemen, one Jewish and the other Polish, guarded the gate which may as well have had carved in stone above it, "Abandon Hope, All Who Enter Here."

All Jews were ordered into the Ghetto – a huge number, about 4,000, a population swelled by refugees from the villages and small towns including the Jews expelled from the large city of Lodz (Litzmanstadt). How could all of us possibly be accommodated in just four or five houses? Several families crowded into a single apartment or even a single room and everyone slept on the floor or in two and three level bunks. My cousin slept in the bathtub and I slept above him on a hastily constructed bunk.

The noose was tightening around our necks but we refused to believe it. At this time our family - our uncles, aunts, cousins as well as other Jews in our town were still alive. But in the short space of seven months almost all of us – 80 percent by the end of 1942 – would be dead.

The Wannsee Conference in Berlin had outlined the plan for the extermination of the Jewish people that was now being implemented. Jewish labor was to be rapidly replaced with non-Jewish labor; the able-bodied were to be sent to concentration camps for slave labor and death by attrition, by hunger and finally by gassing. The General Governor of Poland Hans Frank through his representative to the conference asked that the Jews of his region be expedited first. Representatives of the Nazi treasury, the ministry of interior, the transportation department, as well as the secretary of the office of the Reich chancellery all attended the meeting whose grisly agenda laid out all the necessary plans – including the expeditious disposition of the victims, their transport to the camps and the disposal of their belongings.

In Krosno as elsewhere throughout Poland the *Judenrat* now faced great difficulties in supplying its Ghetto with necessities and people became increasingly desperate. Some tried to escape by acquiring fake Aryan papers and moving to large cities where they wouldn't be recognized. Others, especially women, paid bribes to register as Polish Aryan workers in Germany. Some tried to prepare hiding places in the woods or with Polish friends. Escaping to the forest meant leaving your children and your parents to their fate. It meant surviving the harsh Polish winters without assistance indeed - surrounded by unfriendly, even hostile people.

Escape was fraught with danger for both Jew and Pole. If caught assisting a Jew, a Pole was usually shot sometimes with his entire family or – if lucky – sent to a concentration camp with little chance of surviving. Polish hoodlums referred to as *Szmalcowniks* cruised the streets, movie houses and restaurants and when would-be Aryans were found the *Szmal-*

cowniks extorted money and sometimes even killed them. *Szmalcowniks* also cruised the perimeter of the ghettos and when they discovered Jews illegally scavenging for food the hoodlums robbed them and sometimes turned them over to the Gestapo for a reward. My family knew a rather well-to-do Jewish family in Krosno, the Herzigs, who arranged to go into hiding with their valuables and other possessions. But the Herzigs quickly disappeared for good, murdered it was said by the Polish family that sheltered them and who then took their possessions. Nothing could be done about this as we had no rights, no courts of appeal and no protection.

The story of my own cousin Malka Fruhman is perhaps typical of the fearful treachery of those days when it seemed that qualities like trust ceased to have meaning. A friend promised to hide Malka but this "friend" instead turned Malka over to the Gestapo who shot her without compunction. Many years later Malka's brother told me that Malka's boyfriend, a man named Trenczer, located the traitorous friend in Krosno after the war and avenged my cousin's death.

Many non-Jews, perhaps thousands, put their lives on the line and even lost them in an effort to *save* their Jewish countrymen. But in fact only a small minority of Jews sought to escape the coming Holocaust. The vast majority resigned themselves to the common fate in the Ghetto – not only because of the extreme difficulties involved in escape but also because escape meant abandoning their children, elderly parents and grandparents. There was always a ray of hope that they might be the exception. Otherwise they were ready to share their common fate.

Resettled in Hell: July – August, 1942

At the end of July by my estimate or possibly early August according to others, the Gestapo announced the resettlement of the Jews to the East. They initially requested a '*kontribucja*,' a large sum of money or an equivalent amount of precious valuables in order to postpone the edict. The *Judenrat* scrambled to collect the money to buy a reprieve. After receiving the *kontribucja* the Gestapo allegedly called off the resettlement.

The reprieve was short. About a week later the Gestapo ordered every Jew in Krosno to assemble on a Monday morning in early August at the Targowica, a large plaza used as the cattle market and located near the railroad station on Koleiowa Street. Everybody, regardless of age, gender, or state of health was to show up or be brought there for resettlement. Anyone not obeying orders would be shot on the spot.

Where were we going to be resettled? Would anyone be allowed to remain? Nobody knew. We had heard rumors of such resettlement actions from the large ghettos such as Krakow and Warsaw but only vaguely about their transport to extermination camps. The Gestapo had previously warned the *Judenrat* about spreading such rumors. Anyone found spreading rumors would also be shot.

We held a family meeting together with Moshe Heller the brother of my aunt who was taken in as a junior partner in our business just before the war. Because Moshe and I were young and had frequent contact with the Gestapo it was decided that we should be the ones to go to Gestapo Chief Schmatzler to inquire as to whether the resettlement order applied to us as well since we had outstanding orders from the Germans to fulfill.

We did not wish to be accosted outside the Ghetto so Moshe and I each took a plate of glass and some tools to make it look as if we were going to work. We went to the Gestapo quarters located in a villa that once belonged to the prominent Polish lawyer and patriot Piasecki.[41] We rang the bell and a forty-year-old woman not particularly pretty but with a warm sympathetic smile came to the door. We knew her – she was Hela, an honest country girl who used to work for Mr. Kinderman and was now in the employment of Schmatzler. Hela called him out. Through the open door I saw Gestapo from Krosno and some from Jaslo sitting at a table eating and drinking in a style reminiscent of the Mafia feasts in Chicago. Schmatzler came out still chewing his food, his face ruddy and bloated with booze. He told us that we all had to appear at the assembly point but that we would return to the Ghetto.

We returned home somewhat reassured but not entirely. How could we trust Schmatzler? Yet we wanted to believe him and we knew that we were important to the economy. That's as far as we allowed our thinking to go. In other Ghettos some people were allowed to remain so we hoped the same would be true for us. We agreed that should we be separated we would keep in touch through Joseph Socha, the Polish peasant with the horse and buggy who once hauled glass for us. Later, Joseph did help us to communicate with an uncle from Gorlice and with my brother Schlomo when he worked in Jaslo.

We had no choice but to go but we decided that my mother, sister, and eleven year-old brother Heniek would hide in the attic under some

---

[41] He had been evicted and taken away by the Gestapo together with other prominent Polish patriots at the beginning of the occupation.

dusty old clothes that were stored there. Moshe's wife Rachel and their two-year-old blond curly haired twins also stayed behind. David Fruhman who was handy with tools had constructed a double wall in his house and his parents and my second cousin, David's little boy Michael, went into hiding in there.

The following morning, a Monday, we made our way with the few thousand Jews of the Ghetto to the Targowica. We were allowed to take only about ten kilograms with us and my father and I took glazing tools and some food. Orthodox Jews carried their prayer shawls. A mass of wretched humanity with babies in their arms, in wheelchairs, in wheelbarrows, some on stretchers were making their way to the Targowica as ordered.

It was a very sad and depressing sight.

Hivis, SS volunteers (mostly Ukrainians) were already there as were the Gestapo from Krosno and Jaslo and some Gestapo that I did not recognize and it was the latter that seemed to be mainly in charge. The Ukrainian volunteers had cordoned off the plaza and stood with their machine guns aimed at us. Local Poles kept arriving at the periphery to observe this horrible spectacle. Among them I recognized Mr. Bazentkiewicz who owned the building where my family had our *kitownia* or putty-making shop.[42]

---

[42] Was he there to see us being taken away so he could then take over our shop? Were the others there for a similar purpose? Were they glad to see the Nazis take care of the Jewish problem so they could take over our properties? Didn't the prewar Polish foreign minister Josef Beck declare to the Polish parliament that Poland's problem was too many Jews? Didn't he try to get French-ruled Madagascar to take the Polish Jews? Such frightening thoughts entered my mind at that time. I preferred to give the onlookers

We were ordered to lineup in rows of five. One SS man I did not recognize, whip in hand, ordered the elderly, the handicapped and those on wheelchairs and stretchers to move out of the line to the far corner of the plaza. There was crying and wailing as family members tried to join their loved ones but were beaten with whips and ordered back in line. Those selected were forced onto the waiting trucks, the trucks were covered and SS men with machine guns were stationed on top.

Soon two SS jeeps with mounted machine guns stopped by the plaza to receive their orders. The SS man in charge pointed with his whip dispatching them in a certain direction. Then came a truck with SA men sitting on benches and holding shovels as if presenting arms. It too was ordered to drive off in the same direction. And finally about noon just as the day was beginning to be very hot the trucks with the elderly, weak and very young were ordered to leave in the same direction.

Out of all the chaos and terror of that morning certain images and scenes still come vividly to my mind. One is of a very pretty young girl from Lodz who stubbornly held onto her mother even when she was whipped mercilessly. Her crying was of no avail and she was loaded onto the truck with the others. Another image is Mr. Rieder, a hat-maker who was a neighbor of ours. As he was loaded onto the truck he held his prayer shawl under his arms.

There was chaos, crying and weeping on the plaza. I knew that the dispatched Jews including the pretty girl from Lodz were doomed. The

---

the benefit of the doubt. I preferred to think that they were there out of curiosity and maybe concern for what would happen to us and perhaps to them.

SS men with the shovels would bury them after the machine gunners in the jeeps shot them to death.

After awhile a few among those who remained on the plaza were rounded up by the local Gestapo and brought in line before a table. German employers and some military including an officer from the airbase arrived with lists of their Jewish employees. Jews who worked at the airbase or in the oil refinery were released to their employers and allowed to march off to their jobs. That night they would sleep in the Ghetto or in special barracks built for them at their workstations.

Gestapo Stengler or Stentzler called out names including ours. We were deemed important for the economy and so were each given a blue identification card and allowed to return and remain in the Ghetto.

When we went back home my mother, sister and little brother came out of their hiding places in the attic and we described the scene at Targowica to them. We couldn't talk much though as we were too numb. We were glad to be home but we did not yet know the fate of those left in the plaza.[43] In the afternoon we left the house locking the gate securely behind us and escaped back to the glazing shop where we pretended to be busy on orders for glass. We spent days walking around town with a large plate of glass pretending to deliver orders when in fact we were foraging for food, buying it from Poles we knew in the village.

Most of the people remaining on the Targowica Plaza had to sit on the ground in the heat of the day for hours. Among them were my uncle Abraham and his wife Hencia, their daughters Sarah and Rachel and their

---

[43] It took a day to find out about those taken for execution and a few days to find out about those taken to Belzec.

son Aaron who was just my age as well as Mr. Engel, head of the Krosno *Judenrat*. Later they were marched to the nearby railroad station and loaded into cattle cars. After hours of waiting, the trains, guarded by SS took off headed for the extermination camp whence no one returned. Mr. Engel, head of the Krosno *Judenrat*, was among them.

The following day I managed to have a whispered conversation with Hela the woman who now worked as a maid for Mr. Paes, the SA man. Hela told me that Paes had come home drunk and revealed to her what he had witnessed in a wooded area allegedly near the *shtetl* or village of Brzozow. Paes described how our neighbor Mr. Rieder wrapped himself in his prayer shawl and prayed as he and all the others were shot. According to Hela, Paes found this very funny and laughed uproariously as he told the story.

This came as no surprise yet it was shocking nonetheless. After all we had witnessed the massacre in Dynow a few years before. We were at first less certain about the fate of the Jews transported by train. We learned that those loaded onto the cattle trains – up to a hundred in each wagon – were kept there for hours with no food or water. The train was rumored to have stood waiting many more hours at the Iwonicz station-near Krosno, to allow other traffic to pass.

According to the rumor our family physician, Dr. Baumring, stood at the small wire-covered window of the wagon and begged the SS escort for water. Dr. Baumring was ordered out of the wagon and shot.[44] Considering the death of the resettled in Belzec via slow carbon monoxide gas-

---

[44] I corroborated this rumor about Dr. Baumring when I researched records compiled by Sol Berger from Krosno.

sing from a soviet diesel tank, Dr. Baumring's death by gunshot was a blessing.[45]

About 80 or 90 percent of the Krosno Jews – about thirty-five hundred – perished during this first resettlement action. The total number of Jews remaining in the Krosno Ghetto after August 10th including those working on the airbase and accommodated there in guarded barracks amounted to perhaps 300 to 500 souls. Also must be counted were the 20 or 30 Jews that the SS sought out in their hiding places in the Ghetto and shot. Most of the Jews left in Krosno lost their extended families – without knowing how or where.

Among those who perished were my Uncle Abraham, his wife and three children (Uncle Chaim with his wife Sarah and daughter; Uncle Mordechai, with wife Chana and their two daughters perished later). Gestapo Von Davier shot my Cousin Beila Platner's husband Judah Hausner, on the morning before the Targowica assembly.[46] Of my family only Moshe Heller's wife and two babies, as well as my mother, my sister and my little brother Heniek were given a brief reprieve managing to remain undetected during the SS search of the Ghetto.

The same "resettlement" actions that occurred in Krosno took place in other towns including Jaslo where my Uncle Alter Bialywlos with his wife and six adult sons and daughters as well as other relatives such as

---

[45] We know today that in many instances half of the victims died of suffocation during the transport before even getting to the gas chambers. Carbon monoxide took much longer to work than the cyanide gas widely used later in the war. After gassing by carbon monoxide some victims had to be shot when they were found to be still alive.

[46] Judah used to proffer precious gems to Von Davier for his wife hoping for favored treatment. Von Davier apparently wanted to get rid of a witness before his deportation.

the red-bearded Uncle Henoch with their entire families were extermi-nated. In Dabrowa Tarnowska, my father's town of birth, my father's sis-ter and her husband were killed. They were childless. In Gorlice where my father's youngest brother Sam lived, his wife and one or two children perished. Sam himself had been sent to a forced labor camp in Skarzysko and survived the war in the Concentration Camp of Buchenwald.

In the aftermath of the transport and subsequent massacre in Jaslo, the SS began a clean-up operation. They rounded up about two-dozen young men and women for the job including my younger brother Schlo-mek (Solomon). They had to collect and sort the belongings of the de-ported and killed for shipment to Germany and elsewhere. I was assigned the job of clearing out the homes of the deported victims including the apartment of Dr. Baumring. As I pulled out a drawer of his wife's clothes, I saw two gold earrings hidden between the clothes. While Gestapo Beck-er turned to the next room I stuck the earrings in my pocket and later gave them to my sister. Even today whenever I think about it I feel guilty.[47]

At this time Poles began showing up – trying to extort money from those few who remained of the victims' families. They claimed to have letters from the victims. They also claimed that they had seen them in the East working in the fields. By then we knew that resettlement meant the gas chambers of Belzec. We later learned that a few hundred or so of the elderly and handicapped were killed in a neighboring place near Brzozow. Today we know for certain that all who went to Belzec were gassed –

---

[47] If I had not taken the earrings the Germans surely would have but this fact did not diminish my feeling of guilt. The Poles who broke into the homes of deported Jews to steal their belongings used exactly the same justification. Even in such desperate times was it right to enrich yourself on the misery of the victims?

there was no "selection." SS Commandant Hoess of Belzec later described the prisoners' attempt to break out of the wagons, the dead lying along the railroad tracks and the local people waiting along the tracks to take the clothing and belongings of those who died trying to escape.[48] The victims once they arrived were forced into Belzec's six gas chambers which could hold about five thousand people including crying children and babies. People were bayoneted if they were too slow to enter. Blood was all over the place. Death was slow. It began with the crying and lamenting of thousands of human beings, parents and their children, and ended in complete silence inside the chambers.

Of the Targowica transport there were no survivors. There was only the ceaseless mourning of those who remained.

Hope Abandoned

After August 10th life settled down for a while in the Ghetto. Mr. Kleiner was now chosen as Head of the *Judenrat*. We foraged for food as best we could to supplement the Jewish food ration of about 250 calories a day. But life was not the same after the action of August 10, 1942. It would never be the same again.

The news from the Eastern Front was gloomy again as German troops started their 1942 summer offensive and pushed rapidly through the Steppe to Stalingrad and the Volga River. In the sea battles the German U

---

[48] Hoess' testimony is confirmed by a sole survivor of Belzec. His account, written from prison while he awaited the death sentence was published by the Polish Historical Institute investigating the German crimes committed in Poland and is available from the Polish Museum in Warsaw.

boats were still creating havoc on Allied convoys. Even with our limited access to news from the Allied side, victory looked more encouraging but still remote.[49]

The third week in August we knew for certain that all our families had perished in Belzec. We knew that we had to discuss what to do should another action be ordered. My sister *Mania* – Miriam – who was just a year older than me – decided with typical clear-headed determination to call a family meeting. What should we do if the Nazis tried to separate us and transport us to God knows where? Our immediate family was still intact after the first action of August 10 and we knew now that we needed a plan. To ask a Pole to hide us was difficult. My father wouldn't impose on Mr. Socha who would have been an ideal candidate to ask since he lived in a village but we didn't want to have him risk his own life for us. Of course we didn't know whether he would have even accepted us in the first place. My cousin David Fruhman had asked his closest friend, Mr. Nenski, to hide his five year-old son Michael at his home just outside the city. He declined.

We were living in tremendous anxiety from day to day. We never knew what might happen to us any minute. No one talked about the gassing at Belzec or anywhere else because we couldn't be sure and because it was too frightening to talk about. Feeling the hopelessness of our situation and perhaps with a premonition of what was to come, my sister suggested that my father visit the druggist in our town and ask him for cyanide. Should the Nazis try to separate us from each other she argued, we

---

[49] Furthermore, we didn't believe that the Nazis would allow us to see a final victory and liberation. What could *we* do? That was the question.

should commit suicide rather than be shot or gassed somewhere away from our home.

"No, Mania," I said in the meeting. "Even if only *one* of us survives to tell the story to the world it is worth the risk!" I had to voice my objection to her plan. Was that selfishness on my part or fear of dying? Somehow throughout the long war even with death as my constant companion I had an inner feeling that I would survive.

We let the matter drop.

About two weeks later, toward the end of August, the Gestapo announced through the *Judenrat* now headed by Mr. Kleiner that those who had not shown up on the *Targowica* to receive their blue card would get one if they voluntarily appeared at a certain date and time in front of the *Judenrat* office in the Ghetto. Only a few showed up.

I remember standing behind the door of our house trying to peek through the keyhole at what was going on outside. Suddenly I heard a German Jew, a native of our town, yell out *"Ihr Murderer!"*[50] This was followed by a shot and the man fell dead. I don't remember his name but I can still visualize him today. He was a relative of the Schildkraut family from Krosno who had been deported from Germany and dumped on the Polish border in 1938.

This strategy of luring out those in hiding was all too successful.

One day a few weeks later the *Judenrat* assigned me and a small group of others to duty at the oil refinery in Jedlicze.[51] We left for the re-

---

[50] You murderers!
[51] Very few Jews remained in Krosno. In the labor shortage created by the exterminations, we were taken out from our shop to supplement the work force.

finery early in the morning. When I returned home that evening I found my father crying and tearing out his hair. My little brother Heniek was also crying. I had never seen my father cry before and I knew instantly that something terrible had happened.

"Where is my mother?" I cried. "Where is my sister?"

They had grown tired of hiding and had fallen for one of the Gestapo's ploys. Thinking they would be given as promised, a blue card, they were loaded on trucks and driven off in the direction of Jaslo. I was furious with my father for letting them out when I was not home. I screamed at him. I became hysterical, crying and yelling.

"Why are you pouring salt on my wounds?" My father cried.

I wanted to run to see Mr. Paes to find out from him where they were taken and ask him to help me get them back but it was after curfew and I couldn't leave the Ghetto.

I managed to find out what happened from Moshe Heller's wife Rachel. Rachel had gone with my mother and sister that day but Rachel had somehow escaped from the transport and slipped back into the Ghetto. Apparently a few dozen Jews were loaded on trucks and driven away in the direction of Jaslo but the truck blew a tire outside the city and everyone was ordered to disembark and wait until the tire was repaired. A number of village peasants were returning by the same road to Krosno so Rachel slipped unnoticed from the group and attached herself to the peasants returning to the city. She told us that my mother approached Gestapo chief Schmatzler who knew my mother and reminded him that she is the glazier-master's wife. Schmatzler slapped her in the face and told her to stand back with the group. According to Rachel the transport was going in the direction of Jaslo.

Early the following morning I went to see Paes.

"It's too late now," he said. "Had you come to me the day before I would have told you the Gestapo had ordered trucks."

It was too late. Rumors abounded: They were put in jail in Jaslo and they were put to work in this or that place. But the peasants of the village of Moderowka on the road to Jaslo were the most reliable witnesses. They said that the transport was driven to a wooded area there and they were shot and fell into a mass grave.[52] Given what we knew it was plausible. I have been back in Poland a number of times and visited the area. There are a number of mass graves there as well as multiple crosses where Poles had been shot. A peasant living across the road who was then a youngster told me that the Nazis brought Poles from the Jails, from the concentration camp in nearby Szebnie as well as Jews from Krosno and small towns in the vicinity such as Frysztak and they shot them there. He remembered that after the shootings the SS men came to his home across the road to wash up and clean blood off their clothes as their outdoor well.[53] I queried the peasant as to the approximate time of this particular transport – the end of August and beginning of September – and he remembered the killing. According to the peasant, villagers searched for valuables along the road that the victims in anticipation of their fate had thrown away.

---

[52] The Rabbi of Krosno, Samuel Fuehrer and his son-in-law were allegedly also on that transport.

[53] There were supposedly mass graves in other villages including the mass grave where the 5,000 Soviet prisoners of war were killed.

I could do nothing. After my initial outburst of emotion I felt nothing. Numbness settled over me and seemed to last for the duration of the war. It was perhaps the only way I could manage to live through the sudden bursts of violence and deadening humiliation occurring all around me. I apologized to my father for yelling at him and life went on. I think my mother's disappearance was especially hard on Heniek who was only eleven. Who was left to comfort him? We scavenged for food and tried to survive. It was just a matter of time before our time would come. Another Polish glass shop opened in Krosno and took over our glass beveling shop and most of the work we used to do for the Germans. For all practical purposes we still went to the shop on Ordynacka Street – it was more secure than the Ghetto – but we had little to do there.

The Liquidation of the Krosno Ghetto (1942-1943)

On December 4th, 1942 the Ghetto was liquidated and Krosno was made *"Judenfrei,"* free of Jews.

On a Thursday afternoon, December 3, 1942 the order went out for all Jews to assemble the following morning, Friday, on the Ghetto street where the small egg and poultry market once stood. What would we do now? We wondered. This time we thought that probably none of the Jews would remain in the town. We had a meeting with Moshe and his wife Rachel and decided to spend the night hiding in the cellar of our shop outside the Ghetto. The following morning we would see what was happening.

Our small group included my father and I with my little brother Heniek still longing for his mother and Moshe Heller with Rachel and his two little children. We all put on our best warm clothes and slipped out of the Ghetto to our shop on the Ordynacka Street. Once inside the shop we lifted up a cover which led via a ladder to a cellar. We settled for the night there. Needless to say we didn't sleep a minute and had to be quiet and hold the mouths of the babies if they should start crying in order to not be heard by a neighbor upstairs who might give us away. We spent an awful night in the cold damp cellar.

Around six o'clock in the morning we decided that Moshe would take a plate of glass and walk out to see what was going on. He immediately returned with the news that Ukrainian *Hivis* with machine guns now surrounded the Ghetto. What do we do now? What is going to happen to the Jews in the Ghetto, are they going to be shot?

We had no choice. We decided to wait until the ethnic German trustee opened the shop. My Uncle Sam who had been his neighbor had written us that this German was trustworthy. At eight in the morning we heard him arrive in the store. We lifted the cover of the cellar and crawled out. He appeared shocked to see us all there.

"What are you doing here?" he asked.

"We didn't know what to do, we were desperate and so we came here." "The Ghetto is surrounded by *Hivis* with machine guns."

"You cannot stay here," he said. But he offered to go toward the Ghetto and see what was going on there. We hoped that he would come back and tell us that not all Jews had to leave, to reassure us that because we were important to the economy we might be able to stay. He soon returned and to our great shock he had Gestapo Becker with him. Becker told us to follow him into the Ghetto and we had no choice but to do so.[54] As we arrived in the Ghetto the Jews were all there already lined up outside with Gestapo men from Krosno and Jaslo as well as *Hivis* among them. Becker told us to go to into our homes and get some clothes and come right out and line up with the others.

We got into the house, threw a few items in a pillowcase and lined up on the street as ordered. I remembered that a Polish acquaintance of my family's had given me a goose that day before and I still had it so before going back out I took the goose and shoved it under the bed. Uncle Chaim and Mordechai with their wives went back into their hiding places between the two walls that Dave and Black Joe had built for them.

This time the local Gestapo from Krosno and Jaslo were in charge. The Ukrainian *Hivis* with their machine guns formed a ring around the Ghetto and some also stood inside the Ghetto holding us hostage.

The savagery began.

First, a sled was pulled into the plaza. Sitting on it was a young woman whose crime against the Master Race I will never know and whom I did not recognize. Someone near me said she was from Rymanow, a nearby *shtetl*. Next, the head of the Jaslo Gestapo, a man named von Raschwitz, stood before us and ordered the sled turned in such a way that the young woman, now shaking and crying, faced away from them. The-

---

[54] Deep down we knew all along that we would have to return to the Ghetto. It was good that we were found, actually, because if we had been found later we would have been shot on the spot.

reupon, he took the carbine from a *Hivi* and shot her point-blank in the back of the head.

This atrocity immediately triggered others. Becker began a shooting rampage. When the Tepper family arrived, apparently late, Becker had them placed against a wall and shot. A teenager my age from the village of Turaszowka who was an apprentice in Mr. Koenig's sweet bakery came out in his working white jacket. Becker likewise placed him against the wall and shot him. There were more shootings but I didn't see them all.

Then three young men – boys really – appeared. Two of them were the sons of Bogen the bookbinder. The other I recognized as Berish Wilner. As they came down, Becker – in a fury at latecomers – lined them up against the wall. He first shot the Bogen boys; then Berish Wilner's time came. Suddenly Berish turned around and waved a sheet of paper at Becker. Becker read it and let him line up with the living.[55]

Some Gestapo men went into the houses searching for Jews. Gestapo Hauch entered the house of Mrs. Presser a former neighbor of ours who was sick and bedridden. I could see him going into her house and I feared that he would find her. Indeed, a minute later, I heard a scream and a shot. There were more shootings both inside and outside the houses.

---

[55]After the war when I was visiting Tel-Aviv I had a conversation with Berish Wilner about that morning in 1942. He told me that he had been hiding with the Bogen boys in the attic. Through a crack in the wall the boys observed what went on below. When they saw Becker bring us in from the outside they became convinced that probably no Jew would remain in the Ghetto. They decided to come down and line up. The piece of paper Becker held in his hand was a letter certifying that he worked for the Kirchhof Company. "What do you think made Becker change his mind and not shoot you?" I asked him. He answered, "Becker had already done his deed for the day."

Schmatzler now marched alongside our lined up rows and took out about two-dozen of us including my father, me, Moshe Heller; Mr. Schachner and his workers, the carpenter and a few others who used to do work for the Germans and sat us aside.

We were to go to the labor camp at the airbase; the Schachner group would go to the lumber mill he said. My cousin David could have gone with us but he wouldn't leave his little boy Michael.

My father and I walked over to Schmatzler.

"Please allow my son Heniek to come with us," my father pleaded. "Heniek is eleven now."

"He is still too young," Schmatzler said and he made the same judgment regarding Moshe's children. "But the entire Ghetto is being transferred to the larger Ghetto in Rzeszow"[56] and, pointing to the sky, he added, "They will not go to God in Heaven." And we again allowed ourselves to be reassured by his lie.

"If you agree I will take Heniek and Michael to Rzeszow and care for them there," my cousin David said to us. My father agreed. Since we were to stay in town at the airbase we might be able to assist them in Rzeszow which was only about 40 kilometers away.

The entire group of Jews, lined up in rows of five, was marched out of the Ghetto for the last time. David held the hands of his son Michael and my brother Heniek and Moshe's wife Rachel held her two children in her arms as they marched under the sinister gaze of the SS and armed *Hivis.*

---

[56] Reichshof

The scene was indescribably heart breaking. Heniek was crying, the tears flowing down his cheeks. Heniek had recently lost his mother and now he was being torn from his father and brother as well. Again and again he turned his head back to us as if begging for help. We were all crying. They marched out of the gate and disappeared from my sight.

I never saw them again. The image of their departure is burned into my soul and returns to haunt my dreams and my waking hours.

As soon as they cleared out through the gate I saw Gestapo Hauch from Jaslo leading Moshe's wife Rachel with the two children still in her arms back into the Ghetto. Inside the gate just yards from where I was standing he pulled out his revolver and shot Rachel at point blank range. As she fell, he shot the children. He then bent down, lifted her dress and shot her again probably in her genitalia.

Moshe was standing near me and was about to run to his wife and children but I was able to hold him back. In the shock and unreality of the scene I was able to convince him that the woman who had been killed was not his wife and that the children who had just perished were not his own. This was a family I knew from Rymanow, I lied. There was no sense having him also killed.

Minutes passed. A horse-drawn wagon drove in through the gate. The bodies of the dead, strewn on the ground, were thrown on the wagon and driven away. A wet fine snow began to fall as we stood on the street in the ghetto. We stood like this for several hours, numbed by the snow and by the vision of what we had seen. Finally two airmen arrived and led us to the barracks at the airbase.

That same morning the older people and women and children –
about a hundred souls – were deported from the airbase to Rzeszow along
with the transport from the Ghetto. About a hundred Jews remained at the
airbase and with our two dozen the total came to one-hundred-twenty-
four. The name of the *Luftwaffe* Unit in Krosno was *Fliegerhorstkom-
mandantur* Krosno, *Fliegertechnischeschule* 4. *Luftgaukommando* 8,
Breslau.

The Luftwaffe Labor Camp (1943)

I remained at the Luftwaffe Labor Camp for a little over a year,
from December 4, 1942 to the end of December or early January 1944.
Mr. Langsam, an out-of-town Jew, was the leader there. The *Luftwaffe*
officers in charge of us were *Zahlmeister* 'Warrant Officer' Frankfurter
and above him, *Hauptzahlmeister* Pflauman. Frankfurter was later promoted and became *Oberzahlmeister* Frankfurter. The chief of the airbase
was *Oberst* 'Colonel' Giegold. His deputy was Major Hildebrand who
also served as *Gerichts* or 'Court' officer of the base. A rather wonderful
man named *Hauptman* 'Captain' Hoelzl of Frankfurt served as the sports
officer of the airbase. Captain Hoelzl occasionally came to our barracks to
sit down in our room which was the first room inside the door and talked
to my father. He inquired about our treatment and gave us encouragement
to persevere.

On one occasion he brought news of an Allied bombing raid on
Frankfurt and Hamburg.

"This is happening to us as punishment from God because of what we are doing to your people," he said to my father.

Oberzahlmeister Frankfurter was another fine human being. Initially he claimed that Hitler did not know about what was being done to us and that this was Himmler's doing. Later on he changed his mind as he heard our stories and when he saw the conditions in the Concentration Camp of Szebnie where he drove some of us to pick up our SS provisions.

The barracks at the base was a decent German military barracks with individual rooms with windows and a number of double bunks for sleeping. There was a stove in the center and a table with chairs. Moshe, my father and I were placed in the same room together with Shia Wolf Zafern from Krosno and a Mr. Weinfeld from Gorlice, a town near Krosno, and three people from Lodz.

That same Friday evening that we arrived, Shia Wolf Zafern, a very religious man and Chasid of the Bobover Rabbi, started to pray the Shabbat services in the room.

"What God are you praying to?" I asked him. "Your wife and six children have just been taken away from you and you are blessing your God? Where is your God who allows such horrible acts against the Jewish people?" I said, outraged. Shia Wolf didn't answer but continued praying.

At the airbase we were assigned different duties. My father, Shia Wolf and Mr. Taubenfeld, all from Krosno worked in the enlisted men's basement kitchen usually sorting and peeling potatoes and other vegetables as well as unloading provisions. The redheaded German sergeant in charge of the kitchen was a nice man and frequently gave them food to take back to the barracks. I got ill there in early 1943 with a high fever, delirium and confusion. The camp doctor who had no tools for diagnosis thought it might be pneumonia or typhoid fever. He just didn't know. After about a week or two I started to recover gradually but I was extremely weak. From the kitchen where he worked my father brought back all kinds of tasty food that the sergeant gave him to give to me including *Apfelmuss*, cold refrigerated applesauce and pudding and any number of things that I had never tasted before.

I was as weak as a kitten for several weeks and couldn't stand on my feet without being supported. If this illness had occurred in an SS camp I would have been shot or sent to the gas chamber. When I fully recovered I was assigned to work in the military laundry with a group of Polish girls. They teased me and pushed me onto the piles of laundry. They were nice too and shared some of their food with me.

Mr. Socha who once transported glass for us happened to be hauling sand to the airbase and brought provisions for us as well as letters from my father's brother, Uncle Samuel in Gorlice who worked in a labor camp at an ammunition factory in Skarzysko and from my brother Schlomo who worked with the labor group in Jaslo cleaning and sorting out the clothes of the Jewish victims from Jaslo and surrounding towns. Through the cart driver Socha we also received one letter from the Rzeszow Ghetto that David managed to smuggle out.

In February, 1943 all communication from my brother in Jaslo stopped. We feared that something had happened. His last message to us concerned two girls from the Tailor shop at the *Hivis* camp in Szebnie. The message said that Chana Diamant from Krosno and Lola from Lodz –

she was my girlfriend in the Ghetto – were imprisoned in Jaslo after trying to escape across the border to Hungary with two Ukrainian Hivis.

About this time the Gestapo in Krosno sent a communication to the Luftwaffe requesting that Moshe and I glaze a certain building that was once owned by Mr. Dym in the former Ghetto and that was now being re-novated by the SS for the office of the *Rassenforschungsinstitute*.[57] The *Obersturmfuehrer* in charge of the Institute was to take us first to Jaslo to pick up the glass for the windows. This presented an opportunity to see my brother.

When we arrived in Jaslo I approached the *Obersturmfuehrer* and he promised to find out from the Jaslo Gestapo about my brother. When he returned he told us that my brother wasn't there anymore and his whe-reabouts were unknown. We didn't get to see the others working there either. We feared the worst and never heard from my brother again.[58]

That same month of February 1943 we learned of the defeat of the German Sixth Army under the hastily promoted to *Fieldmarshal* General von Paulus. Nearly 500,000 German troops were lost. Soon thereafter we also learned of the German defeat at the largest tank battle at Kursk for-cing the Germans to retreat. The Germans reported it as a "planned re-

---

[57] Race Research Institute

[58] It was not until I met Frieda Fraenkel at Schindler's camp that I learned he wasn't alive. Frieda refused to give me any details until long after the war. Apparently my brother had access to the outside on glazing jobs including the jail and knew the Polish jailer. My brother had previously sent us a letter via Socha about the two girls in jail. Someone saw him throw a letter in the mailbox and either reported him or a Gestapo man saw him do that. Gestapo Hauch shot him during roll call in front of the Jewish crew there. He warned the others that the same would happen to them if they were caught trying to communicate with the outside. The two girls, Chana and Lola, were also shot. After the war Frieda testified before a German court against Gestapo Hauch. Members and relatives of Hauch's family crowded the courtroom.

treat" to shorten the frontline. These defeats marked the beginning of the end of the glorious German army.

The submarine war was also turning around in 1943 in favor of the Allies.

The Warsaw Ghetto uprising started by a rather small group of Jewish heroes held off the SS for an entire month or longer.[59] Finally, SS General Juergen Stroup, the killing expert from the Lwow Ghetto massacre was called in to take over and the Ghetto was burned to the ground.[60]

At the airbase life went on. Once, *Sturmfuehrer* John or Yohn of the Concentration Camp Krakow-Plaszow came for an unexpected visit. As he inspected our barracks he became furious at the "good life" the Jews were leading there under the protection of the Luftwaffe. *"Die Juden leben da wie Got in Frankreich"*[61] he yelled as he threw photos and pictures off the walls to the ground. He promised a change. He sent three male police officers and one female Jewish police officer from the Krakow-Plaszow Concentration Camp to make sure that we didn't live the life of Riley. At first we didn't trust these new supervisors and slighted them every chance we got. The *Luftwaffe* administration likewise paid no attention to them. They were not very welcomed by either of us. Soon however, the policemen gave up on their mandate to destroy what little contentment we had and joined us in living peaceably and contentedly together.

---

[59] These Jewish heroes who had seen the decimation of the almost one half million Jews in Warsaw were determined to fight even though they had no weapons to speak of.

[60] Stroup was caught after the war and jailed in Poland. A Polish anti-communist journalist shared the cell with him. In a book which the journalist published after his release from prison, he described his conversations with the killer. Stroup expressed no regret at all and said that he would do it all over again if ordered. He was executed in Poland.

[61] "The Jews here live like God in France."

They were happy to be with us instead of at the Concentration Camp in Krakow-Plaszow and we got along well.

By mid 1943 the only members of my immediate family alive were my father and I. My mother and sister had been shot in 1942 at Moderowka. My nineteen-year-old brother Solomon was shot in Jaslo around February 1943. My eleven-year-old brother Heniek died of gassing in Auschwitz together with my cousin David and his five-year-old boy Michael about mid 1943. Of my uncles in Krosno, Chaim Fruhman was shot and his wife died in Rzeszow, my uncle was shot and Aunt Sara died of typhoid fever in the Ghetto there. Their daughter Malka was shot in Krosno when her "friend" gave her away. Uncle Mordechai was shot in Rzeszow and his wife also died in the Rzeszow Ghetto. Beila and Doba, their daughters, were shot in Szebnie. (Their son Red Joe had been shot at the beginning of the war.) Uncle Abraham with his wife Hencia and daughters Sara, Rachel and son Aaron died by gassing in the extermination camp of Belzec during the first resettlement action in August 1942. Their son White Joe was shot together with Red Joe at the beginning of the war.

On my father's side, uncle Alter Bialywlos, his wife and six children were "resettled" from the Jaslo Ghetto and probably died in the gas chambers of Belzec. My father's sister and brother-in-law from Dabrowa Tarnowska were involved in the resettlement action there and were never heard from again. My Uncle Sam who worked in the ammunition factory in Skarzysko and who lost his wife and one or two sons during the action in Gorlice had now been transferred to the Concentration camp of Buchenwald. The only ones remaining alive about the middle of 1943 were my father, Moshe and I in Krakow-Plaszow, Black Joe Fruhman who was now in Auschwitz and Uncle Sam.

After the war Black Joe related to me his experiences in the Camp of Szebnie near Krosno at the time before he was sent to Auschwitz. In 1943 the Camp's commander, *Hauptsturmfuehrer* Kellerman, ordered the liquidation of Camp Szebnie.[62] The camp had already been liquidated earlier in the war when 5,000 Soviet prisoners of war were massacred there after which it became a camp for Poles and Jews. During the first phase of the camp's second liquidation, a transport of 1,000 to 2,000 prisoners was sent to Auschwitz. According to my cousin they had to strip naked with only a jacket on in order to prevent escape from the train. Black Joe was among those loaded on cattle cars and transported to Auschwitz during the winter.[63]

In Auschwitz, my cousin was assigned to work in the BUNA plant of the German "*IG Farbenindustrie*" chemical concern. Conditions were extremely poor there. Periodically the "*Mussulmans,*" as the extremely emaciated were called, were sent for gassing. Joe was tired of living and volunteered to go with such a transport. A physician in the camp whom he had befriended pulled him off the truck and spared him. He eventually survived the war in the Concentration Camp of Buchenwald.

---

[62] *Hauptsturmfuehrer* Kellerman later took three favored prisoners and dropped them off in Budapest. At least two of them, the Feuerlichts of Krosno – father and daughter – survived the war. The other members of the Feuerlichts, a rather large family in the egg export business in Krosno had perished earlier in the war. According to a Polish writer imprisoned in Szebnie whose book I read, Kellerman was denounced by some of the SS crew there, brought before an SS court and shot.

[63] About 1,000, who considered themselves "lucky," remained. Among them were Uncle Mordechai's daughters Beila and Doba. Later, the entire 1,000 of them were shot in the nearby forests.

Throughout the rest of 1943 life for us at the airbase was not idyllic but manageable. We were in our own town of Krosno and had contact with Poles working there and at times some of us even ventured into the town by using some of the civilian Germans who would arrange for an airman with a rifle as a guard to accompany us. In this way I would stop by to see Mr. Laskowski, the postwar mayor of Krosno to whom we had entrusted our money prior to the deportation form the Ghetto. I would pick up some money from him and use it to supplement our diet. I even stopped at Savaryn's bakery to buy Neapolitans and other sweets. It was quite risky because if you were caught by the Gestapo you were shot on the spot. Mr. Stryk was shot during such an excursion into town.

Two of our group including Zisie Beim escaped from the airbase into prepared hiding places outside. We were very fearful. If the Gestapo discovered their escape they would shoot some of us for each escapee. Somehow the escape was hushed up. A young man named Mr. Frauwith from Krosno fell ill and was well cared for by some of the female prisoners and by his brother until he died of his prolonged illness.

From time to time when the enlisted men's bathhouse was free we were allowed as a group to take a hot shower there. It felt good coming out of the hot shower into the cold evening air. We didn't know what the future had for us but I was glad to be alive and felt some degree of security while on the airbase.

Toward the end of 1943 the airbase received over 400 Soviet Uzbek prisoners of war for work at the airbase. This concerned us. We were afraid that the SS in Krakow-Plaszow who had merely loaned us to the *Luftwaffe* would cancel the deal and demand our return to the SS. *Ober-*

106

zahlmeister Frankfurter and *Hauptzahlmeister* Pflauman assured us that they would try to keep us. Our anxiety increased when we found out that the entire base and command were to be transferred to the Eastern front and a new unit from the front was to replace them. When a forward administrative command crew showed up to arrange for the takeover they came to our barracks and met Mr. Langsam, our foreman, who assured them that the 124 of us accomplished much more than the 400 Uzbeks who were mainly uneducated and didn't know the German language. The new *Oberzahlmeister* promised to do his best to retain us.

The reassurances were useless. At the end of 1943 the new command took over and the SS duly requested that we be released to them. This coincided with the SS *Reischsfuehrer* Himmler's order that no Jews be employed outside a concentration camp.

At the end of December 1943 we were thus picked up and transferred to the Concentration Camp of Szebnie, now with only a skeleton crew there to clean up after that camp was liquidated. Overnight we found ourselves in radically different conditions. The barracks were horse-stable barracks – unheated and in January were freezing cold. We slept on bunks without any straw to soften the boards. The food was miserable and we were hungry. We were there only for about a week or ten days until the camp was cleaned up and closed. We were packed again on cattle wagons and shipped to the Concentration Camp Krakow-Plaszow in January 1944.

The only bright spot on the horizon was the news that the Soviets were moving rapidly westward and the Allies had chased Rommel out of Africa and landed in Sicily.

The Concentration Camp
of Krakow-Plaszow (1944)

As we arrived at the station of Krakow-Plaszow the SS guards were waiting for us. They marched us to the camp's *"Appelplatz"* for roll call. Here, we were introduced by Deputy Capo Maniek Farber to the head capo Chilewicz, who stood with his whip. Farber told us that the "holiday" at the airbase was over. We would have to adapt to the new conditions here. He spoke with authority. The first greeting I received was a hit in the face by Farber[64] when I approached to ask him whether he would assign my father to work at Mr. Schenker's shoe shop.[65] We were immediately given rakes and shovels to clean the mud and snow on the walkways. We had wooden shoes only, and my feet froze in the wet snow and my earlobes froze in the icy air. This introduction gave us a taste of the camp. Later on we were marched to the bathhouse for delousing and showers and ordered to deliver all valuables.

In the dressing room I saw the corpse of a young woman lying on the bench in the corner.[66]

"Why is there a corpse lying here?" I asked one of the prisoners working there.

---

[64] This was only the second time that I had been hit in the face during the war, the first one occurring in Krosno when I declined a German soldier's order to dump his wash basin. But the atrocities I had been forced to witness were powerful blows of a different kind to my psyche.

[65] We knew Mr. Schenker since he hailed from Krosno and the shoe shop was warm. My father had problems with the tips of his fingers which would get numb and tingling especially in the cold.

[66] I had seen worse – I had seen the brutal murders of Rachel and her children, and of others. Such sights no longer shocked me.

"You guys are lucky coming here in January 1944" he replied.

I stared at him in numb disbelief. I did not feel lucky.

"Berlin has designated this camp a concentration camp as of January." "Now, deaths have to be reported and a report sent to Berlin." "*Hauptsturmfuehrer* Amon Goeth, the Commandant of the camp was shooting people like on a duck-hunt." "Now he has to report the reason for such deaths to Berlin." "This lady's corpse has to wait until a report is made out."[67]

After the showers we were assigned to the barracks number 29. Engelberg was the capo and barracks elder there. The place was a far cry from the airbase barracks. We were fed a watery soup and a slice of bread. Then came our work assignments. Moshe, my father and I were assigned to the glazier and painter shop. To make places for us in the shop some men were reassigned to other less desirable work. We could feel the resentment of the workers there as if we had stolen their positions. It took awhile before we were accepted. There was actually little work to do and we spent most of the day hiding somewhere in order not to stand around in case an SS man or even a capo saw too many of us in the shop.

One of my co-workers was a certain Mr. Farber who by virtue of his family ties (Maniek Farber, the camp deputy, was his nephew) had the status of a *persona grata*. He rarely appeared in the shop and spent most of his time with his wife in the women's barracks. He got his meal rations directly from the kitchen through a back door like all the capos while the

---

[67] We heard stories of Goeth walking or riding his horse around and shooting people at will. My experience and the rumors I heard match the portrait drawn of him by Thomas Keneally in his book *Schindler's List* and by Steven Spielberg in the movie of the same name.

rest of us got a kettle of watery stuff that two of us carried to the shop for dishing out.

Black-marketeering thrived in the camp. Work units assigned to duty outside the camp smuggled in eggs, bacon, bread and other items hidden beneath their clothing, wrapped around the waist or down in their slacks. Certain SS guards, aware of the smuggling, confiscated the goods and sold them to other prisoners. At times they reported the smugglers for punishment. A prisoner allegedly found stealing clothes was hanged in public view on the *Appelplatz* and we all had to march by and turn our heads to observe it.

At five o'clock in the morning we were awakened, dressed and marched out onto the *Appelplatz* for roll call. The barracks capo had us first line up outside the barracks beforehand to make certain that no one was missing. On the *Appelplatz* he would be punished if the count was incorrect. After hearing the barrack capo's report the SS man in charge recounted again and again to make sure. God forbid someone had escaped. This ordeal lasted about an hour. We were then marched off to our workstations.

One day an incident occurred which almost cost me my life. My father and I were sent to glaze windows in a new barracks for the Ukrainian guards outside the inner perimeter of the camp. Through the window of the barracks where we worked I saw a Ukrainian guard in the adjacent barracks hold up a small loaf of bread that he apparently wanted to sell me. I crossed over to his barracks and I was about to enter it when the Ukrainian guard noticed the presence of an SS man nicknamed "*Niedzwiedz*" (the bear) by the prisoners because of his massive bear-like size and gait. *Niedzwiedz* saw me entering the barracks and followed me. The Ukrainian quickly gestured for me to hide under his bunk while he ran up the ladder where he had straw for the horses, feigning business there. When the Bear spotted me under the bed he pulled out his revolver, took aim and told me to stick out my head. I thought that this is the end and I did not want to suffer. My thought at the time was for my father who had probably seen everything through the window.

I stuck out my head.

"*Schade die Kugel*," the Bear said. "Waste of a bullet."

And I began to breathe again as he replaced the revolver in its holster.

"Get out from there!" he ordered me. I got out and stood up.

"Get into there!" he ordered, pointing to an empty room in the next barrack.

I did as he said. He followed me.

"Take your clothes off!" he ordered.

I was not wearing much beyond the uniform of the prisoner but I took it off.

With his whip he started hitting me all over. I ran from corner to corner screaming from pain and he came after me with his whip. This went on for quite a while. Finally he grew tired and started huffing and puffing and that's when he stopped chasing me.

But the ordeal wasn't over. He now took my blouse and started feeling around the collar looking for valuables. He must have had experience in this. He felt something and with his bayonet ripped the collar apart. Out tumbled a five-dollar bill and two single dollars that I had sewn in the collar.

"Aha!," he said and he took out his notebook and wrote down my prisoner number. "Well," he said. "Tomorrow morning on the Appelplatz you will hang for this."

I put my clothes back on and he led me outside to an old well with a chain dangling from it. He threatened to chain me by my neck and lower me down into the well. Just then he noticed a few Nazi children playing around there and he let me go back to the barracks where my father, only pretending now to carry on with the glazing work, was white as a sheet. He had seen all this through the window and was mortified.

Taking out a bottle of schnapps and handing it to me he said that a *Scharfuehrer* who had also seen it through the window gave the schnapps to him with the words "I saw what happened to you son, please give it to him."[68] I stayed awake most of the night dreading what the next day would bring but there was nothing I could do. I didn't tell my father what the Bear threatened in order not to worry him.

The following morning on the *Appelplatz* nothing happened. The Bear probably decided to keep the seven dollars. I told the story to the guys in the shop and the old timers confirmed that the Bear was known for confiscating items from prisoners and selling them for profit. Moshe him-

---

[68] I remember that *Scharfuehrer* very well. He had apparently been transferred to Plaszow from the camp in Tarnow and according to the prisoners from there had been a decent man. I never saw him with a whip like the other SS guards. His face reminded me of Khrushchev's partner Mikoyan with his black mustache and dark complexion. He was a rather quiet man as he walked around the camp.

self later bought eggs from him that he had confiscated from other prisoners.

Sometime later he spotted me in the barracks during the day when I was supposed to be working. He pulled out his bayonet and started poking me in the chest with its tip. I was afraid that he might recognize me. I kept stepping backwards as he followed me with the bayonet and then he let me go.

Around the 7th of May, 1944 a selection took place on the *Appelplatz.*

The prisoners referred to it as the 'Naked Parade.' We had to strip naked and march one by one in front of the Nazi doctor *Hauptsturmfuehrer* Blancke as he sat at a table and directed the prisoners either to the right or left. I was directed to one side with other relatively young healthy looking prisoners but my father and Moshe were directed to the other side. From our shop a healthy painter with psoriasis of the skin and others with hernias and similar visible problems were directed to the other side. My father had always been rather thin with sunken cheeks; Moshe had a low back problem and didn't walk perfectly straight. Such minor imperfections were sufficient to send them to the side of the doomed. Their names and numbers were recorded. The same action was conducted among the women.

My father and I were fully aware what this meant. We were returned to the barracks and hoped for the best. About a week later, around May 14th, my father and the others were deported to Auschwitz. Before being marched away to the cattle train that stood waiting on the rails, my father tried to ease things for me.

"I don't care to live anymore," he said to me, "I have lost everything." "If I live another ten years I will consume another ton of potatoes." He had with him a ten dollar gold coin which he smuggled into the camp and which he gave me even though I pushed it back into his pocket. He would not take it.

I tried to console him – and myself. "Auschwitz doesn't necessarily mean the worst" I said and tried to give him my bread ration for the trip. He pushed it back to me.

"I will not need it anymore, you will." "I pray and hope that you shall survive this war." He had only one wish for me. He told me to be a *mensch*, a good human being. "Don't be stubborn, be considerate of others and be honest" he said.

With this blessing he departed forever.

I still see his silhouette as he disappeared forever from my view. The feeling of devastation was the same as when I lost my mother, sister, and my two brothers, especially my eleven-year-old brother Heniek.

My heart still cries out for them especially in the silence of the night.

I try to fulfill my father's legacy as best I can. I try to be a *mensch*. My father was a hard-working man, only fifty-two years of age. He was as good a human being as one could wish and had to die at the hands of the Nazi murderers and a world of indifferent humanity.

A few weeks later a prisoner brought me a note from the Trencher brothers from Krosno who were imprisoned in Auschwitz. The note said that while they were loading lumber to be shipped to our camp they saw my father and Moshe being marched toward the gas chambers. They put the note between the lumber. Both Trenchers were with us at the airbase and both of them survived the war.

I was now alone, the only survivor of my family.

The days went by. Spring became summer. The Soviets were forcing the German armies to retreat and had already crossed the former Polish border. A number transports were being shipped out from our camp westward. When a fellow from Krosno by the name of Yosek Montag, who used to work for our neighbor Aaron Wallach in his hardware store, came to say good bye to me I took off a sweater I had under my striped outfit and gave it to him since he went into the unknown and I remained for the time being in Krakow.[69]

Transports of Jews from Hungary started arriving as the Regent von Horthy, the benevolent dictator of Hungary[70] was replaced by the Nazis who now occupied Hungary.

Some Hungarian Jews were killed upon their arrival at Krakow-Plaszow. But on one of the transports from Hungary there was a high school girl from Budapest by the name of Alicia, an intelligent brown-eyed brunette whom I got to know a little. I was twenty years old by this time and meeting her I again began a dream of freedom that was less and less likely, but nevertheless I dreamed that if we survived we would seek one another out again. That's all you could do here was dream and dream. And I thought I was dreaming about this time when at mealtimes, we were served something new – a soup called JUS-soup provided supposedly by the Red Cross. It was a noodle soup and tasted delicious. Freedom, love,

---

[69] He didn't survive the war as far as I know.

[70] Von Horthy had refused to deliver the Hungarian Jews to Himmler for extermination.

a family and children were all so remote. Even as the Soviets approached closer and closer and were now only about 100 miles east of us I didn't think that the Nazis would allow us to survive. I had tried many times to imagine myself being selected for gassing or mass shooting – a fate met by everyone of my family. Intellectually I knew it was only a matter of time before my turn would come. Yet somehow even though survival seemed so impossible I had an inner feeling that I would survive this ordeal.[71]

Toward the end of the summer Goeth went on a shooting spree, killing the detested Chief capo Chilewicz, his wife Marysia, Farber – the guy who slapped me and Finkelstein as well as one other capo whose name I no longer recall. Rumors had it that Chilewicz had proffered all kinds of gifts in gold and diamonds to Goeth in exchange for a promise of freedom. Supposedly Goeth made a deal with him. Chilewicz and his wife and a few others were about to be driven in a truck out of the camp but as they arrived at the gate Goeth betrayed them. They were brought to the jail and shot.

Their corpses were laid out on the *Appelplatz* and all prisoners were forced to march by and turn their heads to view them. Signs attached to them read, "This is what happens when you try to escape." They were an ugly sight with flies all over them but I could shed no tears. They treated us horribly and seemed to enjoy their superiority over us.[72] Shortly

---

[71] That's why I had objected to the idea of suicide that my sister suggested in the Ghetto in Krosno.

[72] Their food, quarters and clothes were not the same as ours. They were the privileged class and didn't hesitate to assert their crude rule over us. Their relatives and acquaintances benefited likewise from their privileged status. They received their rations in the

after this SS Camp commander Goeth was dismissed from his post. He had crossed the line even with the SS authorities.

The camp was gradually being liquidated and the inmates shipped out as the Soviets were nearing Krakow.

Around August or September 1944 the order was issued to open the mass graves in the camp and burn the corpses in order to erase any evidence of the atrocities committed there. I was taken out of the glazier-painter shop and assigned to this mournful task. In the sandy soil the corpses were reasonably preserved. As I worked digging with the shovel I tried not to disturb or hurt the corpses. They seemed to me to be almost alive and I was moved by them. I shall never forget one in particular because of what happened.

I was bending down carefully digging out a red-headed man with a baby next to him. He seemed almost to be holding the baby and I was trying not to disturb them in their restful pose. Suddenly a German criminal-capo sent to Krakow from Auschwitz kicked me full force in the face with his boot. It was full of mud and decomposed matter from the corpses. I suddenly saw stars; blood was streaming from my nose and I had dead matter in my eyes, nose and mouth.

I was not working fast enough for him!

Gold teeth and such items found in the mass grave had to be collected and delivered. I found one loose gold tooth in the grave. The capo didn't notice that I stuck it in my pocket and gave it to the goldsmith in the camp. I had again the same guilt feeling as when I had pocketed Dr.

---

kitchen through the back door with the little meat in the kettles spooned out for them from the bottom and we got the water from the top with some grains floating in it.

Baumrings' wife's earrings. I was in the most horrific circumstances and I had nothing, not even enough food to eat and in the knowledge that the Nazis had taken everything from me and my family I found little solace perhaps in taking something of value from one of my own people, like myself a victim. It was something to keep for myself; I don't try to justify myself, only to understand. When I think today about those two episodes I still have a feeling of guilt.

October 15, 1944 my turn came at last. I was assigned to a transport of Schindler's workers who had been brought to our camp from their barracks at Schindler's plant, the Emalia in Krakow. The plant was being moved to Sudetenland. How I came to get on Schindler's List I do not know. Until I heard about Keneally's book based on the story of Mr. Pfeferberg I was not even aware that there was such a list. When I asked Frieda who had worked at the Emalia in Krakow and was later with me in Sudetenland at Schindler's factory whether such a list existed she told me that there was indeed a list.[73]   When I asked Frieda how I got on the list, she said she thought that it was "simply luck." A friend (neighbor of mine in Olympia Fields, Illinois) who first alerted me to the book which he read about in the New York Times had actually asked me that question before I called Frieda about it.

---

[73] The camp secretary Marcel Goldberg apparently once took Frieda off the list. Frieda's boyfriend who was a very nice man and a barracks capo whom she later married discovered that her name had been replaced by someone else's on Marcel's list. The two of them went to see Marcel. She started crying, relating to him that she was the only survivor of her family and had worked at Schindler's factory long before that. He put her back on the list.

"I don't think that this was pure luck," I explained to my neighbor. My opinion is that someone realized that people with different trades should be on the list rather than just professionals and business people. Otherwise how would the camp be built without glaziers, painters and mechanics? Since I was the youngest among the glazier-painters I was placed on the list. When one views the list one finds fake professions. Everybody on the list was marked down as some kind of craftsman when in fact few really were. The rest were protégés of Schindler and Goldberg. 'They needed a 'real one' just in case there was glazing to be done and I was the one."

Today this seems to me a more feasible explanation.

Those going to Oscar Schindler's at Bruennlitz-Bruessau[74] were loaded into a cattle wagon train and sent first to the Concentration Camp of Gross-Rosen in Silesia, Germany.[75] During the trip as I peeked through the upper barbed-wired window or cracks in the side of the car I observed the landscape outside the camps for the first time in a year. I saw people freely standing on the platforms and I envied them. I saw a different world out there. I could tell when we crossed the border into Germany. I noticed the difference in the train stations we passed. The train depots in Germany were more up to date and neatly cobble-stoned; the station buildings and houses neat and painted; quite different from the poorer Polish stations. I remembered from geography at school how our teacher described the West with its houses of side homes. Our villages in Poland

---

[74] Brnenec in Czech.
[75] Now in Poland.

still had many houses with straw roofs, had holes in these roofs for chimneys and had earthen floors.

At last we arrived in Gross-Rosen. The SS guards from the concentration camp were waiting. They lined us up and marched us uphill to the camp. We stood on the *Appelplatz;* were ordered to undress completely and remained there naked in a freezing drizzle. We huddled against one another to keep warm. It got dark and still we stood there. I had with me the American gold coin my father had given me as my inheritance just before his deportation to Auschwitz. I had heard rumors that everyone was searched through and through including the body orifices before going into the showers. So as we waited for our turn to enter the showers for disinfection I dropped the coin to the ground in the darkness.

That was the end of the coin.

We were ordered to enter the anteroom of the showers. There sat prisoners serving as barbers who shaved about an inch wide vertical pass through our scalp and cut the rest of the hair short. The barber shaving my head said not a word to me. I had to kneel down before him and instead of saying anything he simply bumped me on the head to kneel down. Hair shorn I proceeded with the others in line. On each side of me stood a prisoner with a barrel of smelly disinfectant beside him and a broom-like handle whose end was wrapped in a rag that he dipped into it. I lifted my arms, spread my legs and bent over as he smeared each area with the disinfectant. The whole process was deeply humiliating.

Next came the showers. When cold water instead of gas came pouring out I was surprised, relieved and delighted. Minutes before I had wondered whether gas or water was in store for us. It didn't really matter anymore. As were my father and Moshe when they lost everything, I was numbed to pain and I wanted the ordeal to end as speedily as possible. Now my will to live returned.

After the shower we were chased with whips into a barracks-room and told to sit down on the floor bend our knees and spread our legs as wide as possible for the next guy to squeeze in. This was accomplished with the whip. The windows were closed and with the mass of people squeezed tightly like sardines in the small space one felt like suffocating. The windows were finally opened and we could at least breathe. It was impossible however to stand up in this mass and my aching groins and mashed testes made it a nightmare.

We sat like this through the night.

I thought that I could not possibly survive. Dante's inferno seemed like the Garden of Eden in comparison. As the dawn appeared we were ordered to get up (Thank God) and entered a room where clothing of various kinds lay in piles; one pile was shoes, another one shirts – probably the clothing of Jewish victims. Then we ran as fast as possible from pile to pile and picked up a pair of shoes and a shirt. Again the whips got it done fast but we ended up with various sizes. I got two left shoes which I exchanged with another prisoner who happened to get my size and fit.

My shirt was a nightgown that reached to my feet. This came in handy when I developed horrible diarrhea. There was not a shred of paper anywhere so I used strips torn from the gown to clean myself.

Luckily we were there only a couple of days. For me the days of Camp Gross-Rosen were my worst experiences of the war apart from the loss of my family.[76]

Our group was now sent to Schindler's camp in the small town of Bruennlitz located in the east hills of Sudetenland in a picturesque wooded countryside. We received a ration of bread and a small can of condensed milk for the trip and were marched down the hill to the station.

Schindler's Camp (1944 – 1945)

We arrived at Schindler's factory which was under the ostensible command of *Obersturmfuehrer* Leipold who had been transferred from the killing camp in Majdanek near Lublin in Poland.[77] The women assigned to Schindler's camp would not arrive for another two weeks as they were first sent to Auschwitz just as we had first been sent to Gross-Rosen. Each of us was assigned a bunk in a large machine hall. We spent the rest of the day resting and the following day we were assigned our work places.

A certain Mr. Miller from Krakow and I were assigned to a shop in the corner of the factory where the glazing was to be done. It was rather isolated from the main factory buildings where all others worked and it shared a wall with a textile factory where Czechs worked.

High in this wall an opening had been made probably for the belts that in better times drove the textile machines. Having the ability to com-

---

[76] After the war I met a Polish physician in Chicago, Dr. Mianowski, who had been imprisoned in Gross Rosen. He told me that the camp, located in a stone quarry, was known for its cruelty and high death rate.

[77] Mr. Schindler was able to tame Leipold's sadism and kept him in line.

municate with the Czech workers next door was a tremendous advantage. Another advantage of our location was its large, metal, windowless door that seemed to discourage visitors.

At the camp I met two people I knew from Krosno; the mechanical engineer Oscar Gross and Sonia Grajower who spent summers with the Rubins in Krosno. Both Sonia and Oscar had been with me at the airbase in Krosno. On arrival in Krakow-Plaszow, Sonia Grajower and Frieda Fraenkel[78] were assigned to Schindler's Emalia in Krakow. Mr. Miller who worked with me in the glazier shop lived with his wife and son at Schindler's in Bruennlitz. In the Krakow-Plaszow camp he had been a capo. He knew the other capos since most of them (like him) were originally from Krakow. He was a fine person as were his wife and son. We bonded immediately.

To see what went on in the textile factory he would lift me up to peek through the opening in the wall where the Czechs saw me. Soon the Czechs, especially one red-headed fellow, deposited some bread and other food items for us there – a very welcome addition to our bread ration which consisted initially of one-eighth of a small loaf of bread. Miller shared his portion with his wife and son and I shared mine with Sonia, Frieda and Mr. Gross. Sonia and Frieda never forgot my sharing of food with them.

When I got the first ration of bread with some ersatz roasted-grain coffee I consumed the entire portion for breakfast only to learn that this was the ration for the day. From then on I kept this piece of bread in my

---

[78] Frieda, whose married name is Frieda Deutscher, lives in NY and we have stayed in touch.

pocket and just nibbled off crumbs with my teeth. For lunch and supper we got a ladle-spoon of beet soup that was no more than maroon water as far as I could tell. The privileged and the cook's associates got the beets from the bottom of the kettle. The same was true for the grain in the ersatz-coffee.

My urine was maroon from the beets for the initial weeks there. My diet soon improved thanks to Schindler's wife Emilie who managed with her friend Countess Daubek – the owner of a flour mill across the road – to finagle extra flour for us. Thus our bread ration increased from one-eighth to one-sixth and on an occasion to one quarter of the small loaf. I was lucky on occasion to find a piece of horsemeat that happened to float to the surface of the broth.

The food gradually improved. And I was able to add the bounty from the Czechs next door – bread, potatoes, an occasional piece of bacon was put into the niche in the wall. To show our appreciation I began making small objects of metal and glass – small plates whose edges I beveled with a stone, for example. I asked Mr. Gross to make me a drill from a triangular file for drilling holes in the glass and I also got hold of vertical grooved pieces for side arms to make photo stands and metal corners for jewelry boxes. We put these tokens of appreciation in the niche connecting our room with the Czechs'.

There was little for us to do in the camp except for an occasional glazing job. Most of the time I hid with my friends in that isolated corner of ours. Gross visited me whenever possible and Mr. Miller's friends and his son would occasionally get away and spend some time in our pad which became a resort area for relaxing. But we were still on guard. Frequently one of us peeked through the keyhole to make certain that unin-vited guest such as SS Commander Leipold[79] did not pay us an unan-nounced visit.

Around Christmas time 1944, Amon Goeth, dressed in civilian clothes came to visit Mr. Schindler. Apparently he was there to discuss with Schindler his problem with the SS court related to his profiteering in Plaszow.[80]

Everywhere there were rumors that the war was finally coming to an end. The Ardennes offensive of Fieldmarshall von Rundstedt failed after the initial success and the Soviets entered German territory on their march to Berlin.

The young SS guards in our camp were sent to the front and were replaced with guards from the *Volkssturm* – much older men who lacked enthusiasm for the job and thus were rather harmless. One day Oskar Gross came to see me and after swearing me to absolute secrecy told me that Leipold had orders to exterminate us rather than let us go free at the end of the war. Gross organized some trustworthy young men to plan an escape from the camp to the surrounding forests should we receive a sig-nal that would come, I assumed, from Schindler.

I went for it. We were able to scan the surrounding woods since we were assigned to dig anti-tank trenches on the roads outside. An SS guard was just sitting there on a rock peeling an apple and he gave me a piece of the apple. There would have been no problem disarming him.

---

[79] Leipold often walked around the camp with his German shepherd and a young Jewish kid, his protégé.

[80] After the war both Goeth and Leipold were returned to Poland, sentenced to death and executed.

After liberation on May 8th, 1945 we put him in a striped prisoner uniform to protect him from the Soviets who would have certainly made short order of him.

In January Schindler assembled us on the factory floor with the SS guards and Leipold there and gave us a short speech. He emphasized that the war was coming to an end and we shouldn't try to take revenge on the German personnel and guards.

"They did what they were ordered to do as soldiers," he said. He also expressed his regret at the treatment we received and the suffering we had undergone.

Trainloads of emaciated prisoners from other camps were coming to Bruennlitz. Schindler was asked to take these people in since in this chaos no one knew what to do with them or where to take them. Schindler ordered us to start building bunks bedded out with straw and told us to bring a few hundred of those dying people into the camp. They were a sad mass of humanity. Many died as they were being fed and their skin came off as we lifted them but we did everything possible to bring them back to life. Lots of credit for this rescue effort belongs to Emilie Schindler. She was continually present and provided the food and items for the care of these unfortunate dying human skeletons.

Shortly after April 30th news came that Hitler had committed suicide and appointed Admiral Doenitz in charge of his crumbling empire. The killing of Jews was supposed to stop but individual SS men refused to end their four-year killing spree just because the war was almost over.

Schindler prepared to leave for the West away from the oncoming Soviets from the East. He offered those that wanted to go with him to come along. He said goodbye to us and with his entourage left the camp. Leipold was gone. Most guards went home, except for the one we protected.

Some of the young prisoners grabbed the German criminal-capo, the one who kicked me in the face as I was removing bodies from the mass grave at Krakow-Plaszow and taking sweet revenge for his savagery, they hanged him from a pipe on the factory floor. Some of the prisoners during those few anarchic days fashioned a red flag to greet the oncoming Soviet troops who were apparently close to the camp. When a unit of green-uniformed soldiers was seen marching around the periphery of the camp in the direction of the west they ran out with their red flag thinking they were greeting the Soviet troops. All of a sudden the troops unleashed machine-gun fire in our direction. I happened to be in the courtyard and when I heard the shooting I dropped to the ground. They were actually General Vlasov units of Ukrainian SS fighting on the German side. Fortunately no one was hurt.

On May 8th, a very young Soviet soldier on a horse entered the camp. The war was officially over.

Krakow – Plaszow Concentration Camp

K.L.Gross-Rosen- A.L. Brünnlitz/Liste d. männl. Häftlinge,15.4.1945 Blatt 5.

Lfd. Nr.	E.Art u.Nat.	H.Nr.	Name und Vorname	Geburts- datum	Beruf.
241	Ju.Po.	69077	Abraham Selo.	13. 6.28	Tischlergeh.
242	"	8	Beckmann Samuel.	12. 7.24	Futscher.
243	"	69080	Hilfstein Eduard.	17. 9.24	Wasserinst. Ges.
244	"	1	Altmann Dawid.	9. 5.17	Wasserinst. Ges.
245	"	2	Danziker Eduard.	16. 8.09	Konstruktionszeich
246	"	7	Beer Alter.	11.11.11	ang. Metallverarb.
247	"	4	Bau Josef.	18. 6.20	Zeichner/Graphiker
248	"	6	Botner Mjozecz.	2. 5.18	Tischler meister.
249	"	5	Freimann Leib.	15.12.12	Schneidergas.
250	"	7	Gluckmann Siegfried.	4. 4.03	Maschinenbautechn.
251	"	8	Salsam Salomon.	21. 5.06	Maurer.
252	"	69100	Binder Alter.	1.12.07	Lackierermeister.
253	"	1	Baum Juliusz.	7. 7.11	Schuhmachermeister.
254	Ju.Po.	3	Bratkiewicz Motan.	31. 3.09	Stanzer.
255	Ju.Dt.	4	Aububel Dawid.	25. 6.96	Zahnarzt.
256	Ju.Po	5	Beck Friedrich.	3. 4.21	ang. Metallverarb.
257	"	6	Buchsbaum Jakob.	15. 6.24	Tischl.mgeh.
258	"	7	Beder Fischel.	23. 7.25	ang. Metallverarb.
259	"	8	Brenner Jerzy.	4. 5.97	Klempnerei.
260	"	69100	Grubner Chaim.	1. 6.86	ang. Metallverarb.
261	"	1	Blücheisen Mendel.	1. 3.13	Schmiedegas.
262	"	2	Berger Chaim.	21. 7.09	Möbeltischler.
263	"	3	Drieblatt Majer.	10. 6.04	Schreibkraft.
264	"		Abzug Emanuel.	9. 6.25	ang. Metallverarb.
265	"		Bram Rafael.	25.12.99	Schreibkraft.
266	"		Berliner Blau Leui.	7. 5.17	Schlossergas.
267	"		Oestricher Jakob.	11. 7.13	Tischler.
268	"		Baum Naftali.	23. 6.23	ang. Metallverarb.
269	"		Adler Alexander.	4. 6.23	Glaser.
270	"	9	Bialywlos Alexander	26.10.12	Maler-Lackiergas.
271	"	69110	Abusch Josef.	11.11.22	Schlossergas.
272	"	1	Baldinger Isak.	24. 6.23	Wasserinst.Ges.
273	"	2	Herz Dawid.	23. 6.21	ang. Metallverarb.
274	"	3	Curowicz Mai Lech.	13. 6.09	ang. Metallverarb.
275	"	4	Blaufeder Jakob.	31. 7.16	Metzger.
276	"		Blatt Lemcyk.	10.10.21	ang. Autoschanther.
277	"	6	Dringer Dawid.	29. 3.08	ang. Metallverarb.
278	"	7	Kornblau Jakob.	3. 4.17	ang. Metallverarb.
279	"		Goldberg Afreim.	3.12.14	Werkzeugschlossergas
280	"		Grauer Wilhelm.	23. 4.14	Maschinenbauingenieu
281	"	69120	Gros Oskar.	6. 8.17	Schlossergas.
282	"	2	Zukurup Mozan.	6.12.18	Schneidergas.
283	"	3	Koscher Szaja.	11. 5.15	ang. Metallverarb.
284	"	4	Haber Ignacy.	16. 9.18	Maler-Lackierermstr.
285	"	5	Dortheimer Wigdor.	7. 6.23	ang. Metallverarb.
286	"	6	Landesdorfer Izak.	27. 4.09	Elektrikermeister.
287	"	7	Friedman Leon.	1. 8.27	Eisendrehergeh.
288	"		Lejzon Leib.	15. 9.29	Eisendrehergeh.
289	"	9	Lejzon Moses.	15.12.93	Eisendrehermeister.
290	"	69130	Glicenstein Abram.	16. 4.16	Schlossergas.
291	"	1	Hecht Zygmunt.	24.10.12	Tischlergas.
292	"	2	Linkowski Maurycy.	23. 6.05	ang. Metallverarb.
293	"	3	König Jakob.	14. 9.16	ang. Metallverarb.
294	"	4	Goldstein Bernard.	5. 1.03	ang. Metallverarb.
295	"	5	Geller Motio.	16.12.08	Schlossergas.
296	"	6	Dresner Jonas. (Jerek)	4. 9.23	Autoschlossergas.
297	"	7	Friedman Ludwig.	2.11.24	Autoschlossergas.
298	"	69140	Malewer Chaim.	23.12.05	ang. Metallverarb.
299	"	69141	Dresner Juda.	26. 3.95	Stanzer.
300					

Section of SCHINDLER's LIST – I was number 270

L. = list number, Ln. = line number, Rel. = religion, Natn. = nationality,
H. No = prisoner number.

L.	Ln.	Rel.	Natn.	H.No.	Surname	Forname	DOB	Occupation
2	270	Ju.	Po.	69108	BIALYWLOS	Alexander	4.6.23	Glaser

Oscar Schindler in Krakow with his horse

Oscar Schindler with Itzhak Stern after the war

The meeting with Emilie Schindler (bottom, left) circa 1981.
I am at the top left and Inez is at the top right.

PART 4

Liberation and the Return to Poland

Dr. Alex White with Emilie Schindler (circa 1981)
Mrs. Schindler died in 2001 at the age of 93

Oscar Schindler's factory in Bruennlitz
(Germany at the time and now in the Czech Republic)

Liberation and the Return to Poland

When the young Soviet horseman entered our camp on May 8th, the day of our liberation, prisoners conversant in Russian spoke to him. The same day in the afternoon a high-ranking Soviet officer probably a general came to the camp. We prisoners were summoned to hear his speech. Among other things he told us that we ought to thank Comrade Stalin for our liberation. Then he left.

With his departure an almost eerie feeling entered the camp. It was as if the top of our heads had been lifted off. The pent-up fear and rage that we all experienced in response to the terror of that time began to be released and the following day some young prisoners went on a rampage of German homes looting them for clothing and food. I could tell that they felt bad about doing it but they tried to rationalize their feelings by saying things like, "They stole everything from us."

Somehow in the chaos of those first days of liberation – perhaps because my experiences had not been too terrible in the war – I was able to keep a clear head. I recognized the bad feelings I had as disgust for their behavior and I knew their activities were not something in which I wanted to participate. It's true that we lost everything in the war, not just our material possessions but our entire families. But how did we know that this particular German whose house they were looting stole something from the Jews? I asked myself, "Maybe he was another Schindler?"

In the camp the prisoner cooks who had not left with Schindler "requisitioned" a pig from some German farmers living around Bruennlitz and prepared us a delicious soup and some meat. It was the first decent

135

meal we had eaten in a long time. The leaders among the prisoners also distributed some textile materials that the SS had stored in our camp as they were withdrawing. Each of us was given enough material for a suit which upon my return to Krosno I sold. I also received a beige Hitler youth blouse and hat which I put on.

Oscar Gross and I and the girls Frieda Fraenkel and Sonia Grajower discussed our situations. We decided to leave the camp and head for home – if there was still a home. Sonia and Frieda left with the boyfriends they had met at the camp whom they later married. Mr. Gross and others left before I did and only a few people remained in the camp when I set out for my home in Krosno. I took the cloth I had received for the suit, a chunk of bread and a bottle of water and went to the train station. The only identification I had on me was a note distributed by the camp elders certifying that I had been liberated in Bruennlitz and asking the authorities to assist me in my travel home. It was typed both in Czech and German.

I set out wearing the Hitler Youth blouse and shorts I had been given and carrying a satchel with the cloth for the suit and some bread. I hoped to find friends, neighbors and perhaps even family members who had survived the war. I marched to the train station prepared to take any train that could take me in the direction of Prague, the Polish border and finally Krakow. Of course I had no money.

A passenger train arrived and took me only a short distance to a river whose bridge had been destroyed. To get to the other side we had to board a boat. At the other side of the river a freight train stood waiting, it was already loaded with refugees. I climbed on the roof and joined a group of young people already there. The train took off toward Prague.

As it entered a tunnel we had to lie flat in order not to get our heads chopped off. After stopping and going many times we finally made it to Prague.

The train station in Prague was teeming with refugees. I saw an American Red Cross crew dispensing hot soup from a kettle to the refugees. I headed straight for it. The soup was delicious. I will forever remain thankful to them for their help. I sought out a passenger train going to Krakow via Bielsko-Biala at the border on the Polish side. This train was also full of refugees making their way back home to Poland.

On the border Soviet and Polish policemen checked my satchel and tried to confiscate the cloth I had with me. I finally explained to them my situation and they gave me back my treasure. Upon reaching Krakow I inquired and found a Jewish Community center where I received information, assistance and food. The people there strongly advised me not to return to Krosno because of anti-Semitic Polish rightists had killed some Jews there after the end of the war. They suggested that I stay in Krakow until things stabilized. I couldn't comprehend why anyone would want to kill me now especially after I had survived living in hell.

I had to return to Krosno. It was my home. I boarded a freight train to take me via Rzeszow to Krosno. That train stopped in the village of Mecinka near Krosno since the station in Krosno was bombed out.[81] I walked to the main road leading to Krosno and found a peasant with a

---

[81] That area was known to me from the days when I helped my father glaze the windows of the electricity plant there. I recalled having stood on a scaffold there in the winter repairing broken windowpanes with the building swaying from the vibration of the heavy dynamos. My father's fingertips became frozen while we were working there. The putty froze in our hands. It was bitter cold.

horse drawn wagon who offered to take me into town. I recalled the ride I had taken on Mr. Socha's wagon years before. We arrived in town and I almost could not believe where I was. For years I had dreamed of returning home and going straight to Mr. Bergman's bakery and eating every loaf of bread I could find on the shelf there.

But the hunger for human connection with people I had known proved stronger than the hunger for food. I went first in search of Jewish survivors in town. I made my way to the former custodian of our building and inquired about any surviving Jews. He referred me to Mrs. Mania Kalb who and survived with her little daughter in hiding with the help of a Mr. Polujko of Korczyna. She lived in a single room with kitchen in Mr. Dym's house on the Francziszkanska Street in the former Ghetto. With her were a brother-in-law who had survived on fake Aryan papers and his little daughter who had been taken in by a Polish peasant. Across the street from the Dym house in the Fischbein house lived two sisters who also survived in hiding by a peasant.[82]

Both Mrs. Kalb and her brother-in-law were originally Jewish peasants from villages surrounding Krosno. Mrs. Kalb accommodated me in her kitchen. Her little apartment appeared to be the "social center" of all returnees after me. She cooked for us and treated us like her children. She also revealed that a few Jews had indeed been killed after the war allegedly for stealing food from some peasants while hiding in the forests. One of the names I recall was that of the butcher Breitowicz.

---

[82] The two little girls attended public grade school and the children suffered some anti-Semitic indignities from the Polish kids. None of them were going to stay in Poland and were just waiting for an opportunity to emigrate.

Mrs. Kalb was a widow. Her husband had owned a junk shop and had died in 1939 while fighting in the Polish army. Her brother-in-law had the most typical Polish peasant manner of speaking and appearance I had ever seen. I would never have guessed that he was Jewish but he survived only by moving from place to place when other Polish workers suspected him of being Jewish.[83]

They all made their living by purchasing Hungarian cigarettes from Soviet soldiers who smuggled them in across the border and then selling them door to door, a couple of cigarettes here, a few more there - rarely a whole package. I assisted them in the sale and gave them the proceeds. I once tried one of those cigarettes and it set my throat on fire and made me very sick. The Soviet soldiers smoked tobacco called "Mahorka," wrapped in newspaper as cigarette paper was hard to get. It didn't seem to bother them. I saw them during this short time in Krosno devour a loaf of bread with a large onion chewing it like and apple. Those guys could survive under the most primitive conditions. They were used to it.

A week after my return to Krosno, as I returned from selling cigarettes Mrs. Kalb took me to her room for a surprise. There was my first cousin Black Joe Fruhman.

We embraced, crying for joy on one another's shoulder. He had survived the concentration camps of Szebnie, Auschwitz and Buchenwald.[84]

---

[83] They all eventually immigrated illegally to Israel and I visited them there about 15 years ago. I couldn't thank them enough for the care they gave me right after the liberation.

[84] His story of survival also merits a book.

A day later my father's brother from Gorlice, Uncle Sam, showed up with two of his friends, liberated from the Concentration Camp of Buchenwald by General Patton's army and taken back to a Displaced Persons camp in Landsberg near Munich in the American occupational zone. I had seen my Uncle Sam only once when I was about five years old and visited Gorlice with my father. The last time we heard from him was in 1943 via Mr. Socha when he worked as a slave laborer at an ammunition factory in Skarzysko.

Uncle Sam had come to Krosno to see whether any one of us had survived. He himself had lost his entire family. From the Displaced Persons camp in Landsberg in the American zone of occupation he had a certificate asking authorities to assist him in searching for survivors and in making his way back to Landsberg.

Uncle Sam had with him a rucksack full of goodies – all kinds of canned foods, chocolate and American cigarettes which he had received from the multiple American Aid organizations active in the West. We were very impressed with all the goodies unobtainable in the East where no one gave us anything. The items Uncle Sam had – especially the American cigarettes – were worth their value in gold. Uncle Sam's two friends who had also come from the DP camp had similar items but lacked the valuable Certificate of Identification. Black Joe had nothing as he came directly from Buchenwald which was taken over by the Soviets as part of Communist East Germany.

Uncle Sam didn't waste any time with us but pointed out that we must go back with him to his camp in the West and to the Americans. Poland had nothing for us he argued while all kinds of charitable American institutions cared for the refugees in the free West. Just seeing and tasting the goodies from the West was enough to convince us to start preparing to go West while the borders were still open and before the Iron Curtain descended. I was glad I had not registered on my return for the mandatory registration for military service because now I was free to go to the West.

First, we needed to get some money. I sold the material for the suit. We sold our putty forming machine to Mr. Bazentkiewicz and the beveling shop to the glazer in town. At the beginning of the war Black Joe and I had buried some silver pieces belonging to Uncle Joseph in our cellar in the ghetto. Dr. Hodunko, a Ukrainian physician in Krosno to whom we had entrusted our Uncle Joseph's new furniture paid us for the latter. In these ways we accumulated a little money. Not much but a little.

Uncle Sam and his two friends suggested that we buy American Occupational Dollars called script from the returning Polish refugees from the West and sell it on the black market to American GIs. Each one of us got a small piece of luggage in which my cousin and the others fashioned a double bottom for hiding the script. We put a few rags in the luggage – we didn't own anything anyway – and set out for Gorlice.[85]

We left late at night hoping by that time the border police would be asleep. If not, a package of American cigarettes would compel him to allow us passage. We hired a peasant with a horse drawn buggy to take us –

---

[85] Uncle Sam's hometown, on the border with Czechoslovakia. Border town mayors were authorized to issue permits to cross the border up to 15 kilometers to search for relatives and Uncle Sam planned to take advantage of his acquaintance with the mayor of Gorlice to obtain permits for us all. A single package of American cigarettes did the trick.

not just 15 kilometers across the border but about 30 to 40 kilometers across as far as Bardjow, a large town in Slovakia, where we had some distant relatives in the wine business who might be able to help us get through to the West. At the home of these relatives we met Mendel Schwebel and Pinia Thaler, two young men from Krosno about my age who had survived the war with the help of a custodian of the bank in Krosno by hiding in the cellar under the garage of the Slowacka Street bank. They too were relatives of the wine people in Bardjow.

Our relatives fed us, bought us train tickets and on the following day took us to the train station. Here we stood out in the scant crowd and two policemen stopped us and asked to see our papers. Since we only had the 15-kilometer permit we were accused of being Polish spies and taken to the police station and thrown into a cold cellar. The following morning after interrogation we were put into a horse drawn wagon (under police guard) who was supposed to take us back to Poland.

Here the American cigarettes again came in handy. My uncle gave the policeman a package of Chesterfields and he told us to disappear. We went back to the wine people in town who took us to a larger city, Kosice, where we wouldn't be so conspicuous. At the busy crowded train station in Kosice we had no problem boarding the train in the direction of Karlsbad[86] and the western border of Czechoslovakia with West Germany. It was an all-day ride.

As evening came and darkness fell we approached the demarcation line between the Soviet and American sectors of Western Czechoslovakia.

---

[86] Karlowe Vary

In the dark wagon we were the only passengers with our small double bottom suitcases. Just before the demarcation line a pair of policemen, one Czech and one Soviet, boarded the train. With their flashlight on us they demanded our identification papers.

My uncle and I showed the policeman our camp certificates. My cousin Black Joe and my uncle's two friends from Gorlice had no identification papers and so at the next station they were asked to exit the train. They went out onto the platform leaving behind the luggage with the script hidden in the false bottoms. My uncle and I were allowed to continue. We didn't know exactly where we were but we knew that we were heading west toward the border. Around midnight the train stopped at the end station and fewer than half a dozen people (including my uncle and me) got off.

Two policemen were at the station.[87] They took my uncle and me inside. We were now burdened with the other friends and my cousin's luggage. Not that it weighed anything but we were concerned about the script hidden there. After we showed the policemen our certificates they asked us to open the luggage. They must have had experience with smugglers although I doubt that they suspected us of being professionals. As we opened the luggage they took out pocketknives and went straight for the double bottoms with all the script. There was little talking since we didn't understand Czech.

---

[87] As we were standing in the station, we caught a fleeting glimpse of some strange green-uniformed soldiers who were unfamiliar and hence unrecognizable as the American GIs they were.

They took out the script money and started counting it and then wrote a long report and had us sign it. It didn't matter since we didn't know what we were signing anyway. They took the money with them and disappeared leaving us there for the night.

We sat there for about three or four hours seeing no one and hearing nothing. We decided to walk outside and see whether there was anybody around. There was not a light or a human being in sight. We decided to skip before they returned and jailed us.

We assumed that since the train had stopped on the border that West Germany must be ahead and started walking through the fields in that direction. We had no luggage with us so it was easy. Dawn was just starting and at a distance we saw a man with a white armband identifying him as a German.[88] We approached him for directions to West Germany.

To our surprise he told us that we were just coming from West German territory and were now on Czech territory. He directed us to return and go in the opposite direction toward the small town of Cham. I was so grateful to him that I took off my mother's watch and gave it to him. It was stupid of me to give up the only possession dear to me but I was so grateful to him that I didn't think.

We reached what appeared to be a main road and walked parallel to the road trying to hide among the trees and brush of the forest. Whenever we heard the sound of a jeep coming in our direction I told my uncle to drop on the ground so as not to be seen from the road. We finally came into town. We found a German Relief Office for returning German politi-

---

[88] The Czechs had the Germans wear white armbands just as the Germans had the Jews do.

cal concentration camp inmates. We went in, registered and were given accommodations in a small hotel for the night as well as coupons for meals and train tickets to the large city of Regensburg on the Danube.

On our arrival in Regensburg we sought out the Jewish Refugee Committee Center where we looked for any returnee we might know. We found out that the Beim brothers from my hometown were there and that the Head of the Committee was a Krosno fellow by the name of Judah Salomon. To see Judah was virtually impossible. There were crowds of people standing in line to see him for all kinds of things. We found one of the Beim brothers and he accompanied us to their room in an apartment which a German family shared with them

The following day we continued by train to the Displaced Persons camp at Landsberg on the Lech River. Young Jewish kids on the train, probably from some refugee camp, were singing songs to the annoyance of the German passengers. I struck up a conversation with a German passenger who complained to me about the Americans[89] who were eating their food and leaving nothing for the Germans. I told him of my experience with his countrymen and he fell silent.

The Displaced Persons Camp in Landsberg was in a former German SS compound. There were a number of large buildings serving as living quarters, kitchen and dining halls. My uncle and I went straight to his previous living quarters which he had shared with a number of people including his friends who had been taken off the train. They were for the

---

[89] The 'Amis,' he called them.

145

most part people who worked with my uncle in Skarzysko and were liberated by Patton's army in Buchenwald.[90]

One man in the room was a small chondroplastic short male with markedly bowed legs who was a cobbler and survived the concentration camp as a sort of Nazi mascot singing songs and repairing the Nazi's shoes. He was quite funny and to the Germans in the camp probably a Marionette.[91]

The entire camp was run democratically by the Jewish residents with supervision from the American Jewish Joint Distribution Committee (AJDC). The refugees had organized various associations including political and Zionist groups and the place was as busy as a beehive. There was a hospital with a number of Jewish physicians and an American physician in military uniform at the head. Three meals were provided daily in the large dining room. It was here that I tasted American ketchup for the first time in my life. I liked it on bread so much that I thought that the inventor deserved the Nobel Prize. I registered as a member of the camp and received a ration card as well as immunizations against common infectious diseases and the chance to stand in line with the others for food and clothing. A new life was beginning for me.

About two days later who should appear but my cousin Black Joe and my uncle's two friends who had been taken off the train.[92] They im-

---

[90] The latter was considered the mildest of all other concentration camps although when General Patton, Eisenhower and Bradley had visited the camp there were piles of dead emaciated skeletons lying around which the fleeing guards had no time to incinerate.

[91] Kasperl in Bavarian-German

[9292] They had been taken to Karlsbad and released and thus were quickly able to make their way back across the border in the company of other Jews in the same predicament.

mediately wanted to know what happened to the luggage they had left with us on the train. My uncle and I explained. Black Joe of course believed us but my uncle's two friends led by the older one whose first name was Manis didn't believe the story. They accused me in particular of having stolen their money.

I was furious! I was angry that they did not believe me and I was angry that they had even burdened us with their luggage in the first place instead of taking it themselves. I was so angry I could have grabbed a chair and broken it over Manis' head. He kept up a tirade against me in front of the others in the room demanding that I go to the local resident orthodox Hungarian Rabbi and swear by the Bible that I had not taken their script. I hesitated to go but my uncle and cousin persuaded me if only to shut Manis up. I went to the Rabbi and swore by the Bible but even that did not seem to convince Manis. I thought of what my father used to say - the truth eventually comes out.

My uncle came to visit me in Munich about two years later and told me that two Jewish fellows came to the camp looking for Samuel and Alexander Bialywlos. Manis and his friend were there and wanted to know from the men what this was all about. The men told them that money had been taken away from the two Bialywlos' at the border and they had lawyers who for a fee could retrieve the money. Manis and his friend jumped up telling the men that this was *their* money.

"It may have been your money," the two men told Manis, "but we need signatures of Samuel and Alexander Bialywlos, the original signatories authorizing us to retrieve the money."

"Why should I sign?" I told my uncle. "I'd rather sacrifice my part and deprive Manis from getting his as well." That's how angry I was with Manis and his friend. They had accused and insulted me and as a Jewish saying goes, "Better to sacrifice and burn the bed as long as the bed bugs perish with it."

My uncle pleaded with me so I signed on the condition that Manis give a donation to charity. In the end I got fifty dollars from my uncle; Manis and my cousin got 100 each. I had the least amount of money to begin with so that was all right with me. I guarded that fifty dollars in my pocket like the ball of my eye and waited to exchange it on the black market for German marks to buy myself a Leica camera to take with me to the United States when I emigrated.

I befriended at this time a man named Jacob, a Jew from a village near Krosno who had returned from Siberia after the war. Jacob – or Yankele as I called him in Yiddish – dealt in the black market on the Mehlstrasse in Munich as was very common at this time. He gave me the name of a friend of his, a black marketer in currency who would give me, as Jacob's friend, a good deal. When I was ready to exchange the money I sought out the dealer on the Mehlstrasse. I gave him my treasured 50-dollar bill; he scrutinized it for a few seconds, stuck his long dirty thumbnail under the zero and pulled it off. It was only a five-dollar bill with a zero pasted on.

My disappointment was keen as you can imagine.[93] But my friend Yankele when he heard what had happened gave me a Kodak Retina 2 camera as a gift.

But that was two years after I arrived at the Landsberg Displaced Persons camp.

In the first months in the camp my cousin Black Joe and I began to come alive again. Black Joe, a locksmith mechanic by trade found a way to teach at the ORT trade school in Landsberg. I knew that I too wanted to move forward with my life but I wanted to do better than simply use my trade skills as a glazier. I was extremely hungry for an education so with the support of my Uncle I went to the high school in Landsberg and asked for help with my education. I was introduced to two teachers, one in history and literature and one in math and the natural sciences who consented to give me private lessons. In exchange I paid them with cigarettes, white bread, un-roasted coffee, salami and canned goods from the CARE packages and camp rations we received.[94]

---

[93] I was reminded of a funny story I heard years ago about a rabbi who was known to take bribes. He would take his sandals off and leave one on each side of his feet before hearing sides in a dispute between two litigants. The shoe with the money in it let the rabbi know which litigant he should favor in a case. Once, a litigant tricked the judge by putting metal pieces in the shoe instead of coins. He won the case. "This world is full of thieves," the Rabbi hollered when he took off the shoe and discovered the fake coins.

[94] I was especially grateful to my uncle for his support because of the illness he suffered at this time. In Feldafing near Munich he was hospitalized in a sanatorium for tuberculosis acquired in a malnourished state in the concentration camp. I visited him there frequently and the doctors and nurses loved him and gave him the best care.

The two high school professors were very pleased with my progress and my rapid acquisition of knowledge. After a year they issued me a Certificate of Maturity.[95]

I was busy studying and planning to sign up at the University of Munich. I met a few students in the DP camp who planned to do likewise as soon as one of the universities reopened and began offering courses again. I couldn't wait to start studying at the University. It almost didn't matter what field I studied. Medicine however was my first choice. At the Landsberg camp we were referred to the American Jewish Joint Distribution Committee (AJDC) office in Munich for assistance. Professor Joslin, a sociologist from New York University, was head of the Education Department. I obtained an interview with him and after a while he gave me some forms to fill out and have signed by my professors. I would also have to undergo an examination of maturity by the American physician in charge of the hospital in Landsberg.

At the same time I learned that a Jewish Students Union was forming in Munich with offices on the Grilparzerstrasse. I went to Munich and joined the group.

The medical faculty had not yet opened but the architecture school in Passing, a suburb of Munich that had not been bombed, was accepting applications. I was so anxious to start anything that I went there and obtained an application. In the meantime I heard that the medical faculty at the university was to open soon.

---

[95] In Europe a "Matura" is the equivalent of a high school diploma for eligibility to enter a University.

I went to see Dr. Joslin again armed with all my credentials. He reviewed those and gave me a letter for the Dean at the University of Munich. With my uncle who had been with me everywhere since his release from the sanatorium, we went to the Dean's office at the University. In the waiting room there we struck up a conversation with another student waiting there for the same reason. I will refer to him as John from Budapest. He had already completed one semester of medicine in Budapest before being deported with other Jews from Hungary. Later he was liberated in Bergen-Belsen and went to live in a DP camp in Bavaria.

John was called in first and after about a half hour interview he came out with a note to the Registrar, Mr. Flachslander, for admission to study medicine. My interview went as well as John's and we both decided to start looking together for a place to live in Munich. We made our way to the city Wohnungsamt[96] where we were given a number of addresses. The people were not very happy to see us foreigners but in the end they decided to give preference to young singles rather than having to take in families later. I got a room in Nymphenburg and John got one within walking distance from mine. My building had not been bombed out and I moved into a room in an apartment with a childless young family and their older mother. I was not greeted with great enthusiasm but we lived a peaceful coexistence. I liked the city of Munich.

John and I studied together and exchanged lecture notes. Through him I met other Hungarians. One of them, a young man by the name of Tommy, was quite a character. He worked for the AJDC and wore an

---

[96] Quartering office

American uniform which gave him status and prestige. He knew some English and would twist his tongue to imitate an American. He had no problem getting a good large apartment in the Borstei, a large complex of buildings built in the 1930's with modern kitchens and bathrooms. John and I eventually moved in with him since most of the time he was not there.

The premed studies went well. Chemistry, Physics, Zoology, Botany, Anatomy, Physiology, Physiological Chemistry, Biology, Comparative Anatomy of the Vertebrate, Topographic Anatomy and Microscopic Anatomy were squeezed together without a recess in order to catch up due to the late opening. The first three semesters were compressed into the first year. I absorbed the stuff like a hungry animal.

In the Anatomical Practicum and section John and I were paired with two Bavarian girl students and worked on the dissection of a corpse. We became close friends and often spent our weekends on outings with them. One of the girls came from a farm and so she was able to bring us cuts of meat and other foods from time to time. Food was closely rationed; the black market was rampant but we didn't have the money to buy there. Once one of the girls named Resl got up at four in the morning to stand in line for a ration of meat. She brought home an entire jaw of a cow with all its teeth in it. As the group's unofficial cook I prepared a meal with it – first cooking the hell out of it for broth for soup.

I took my medical exams and passed with top grades before starting my clinical years. My Hungarian friend John left for the United States under a scholarship. I missed his friendship after he left but I made new friends and remained close with the Bavarian students. We studied, took exams and enjoyed our free time together. My Bavarian women friends had spent a lot of time in the large city of Munich so they were able to introduce a small town boy like me to a variety of cultural institutions. We attended wonderful concerts directed by the famous symphony directors as well as opera and we visited the museums regularly. With our student identification cards these events cost only pennies.[97] All of the exposure to culture helped me cope with my experiences of the tragic war years and the loss of my family. My uncle and my friends substituted at least partially for my lost family.

My primary goal at this time was to build a future for myself – not in Europe but in the United States. When my Hungarian friend went to the United States to study medicine I began to dream of this possibility for myself. But when a few years later one of my Bavarian women friends also immigrated to the United States to serve her internship I became even more impatient, sitting on pins, waiting to join my friends across the Atlantic.[98] I would leave for New York as soon as my immigration papers were approved. While I waited I looked forward to a future in the United States and the hopes I held in this dream gave me the strength to persevere until June 8, 1950 when I arrived in the United States on the Liberty ship Admiral Sturgis.

---

[97] My hometown of Krosno had none of this kind of culture. But even if it had, as a youngster from an orthodox home, I would not have been exposed to it. Of course I was only sixteen when the war broke out and time stopped for me – too young to appreciate this kind of culture.

[98] These friends were also invaluable to me when I did arrive in New York. Within one week's time of my arrival I had started to serve my internship in New York where an older medical intern who was a friend of mine had given me an introduction.

Uncle Sam in 1946 (Left) and later
in the United States (Above)

1946 in Straubing, Germany with a survivor cousin of my father (center with black sweater). I am to the right of her (partially hidden).

Dr. White (left) in Munich in 1945 and later with fellow Interns (below – fourth from left, top row) at the Lebanon Hospital in the Bronx, New York City

With other Holocaust survivors, 1950

Munich 1947

With fellow medical student, Alex Barnet – Munich, 1948

Munich   1946 - 1950

Our wedding - February 28, 1953

Epilogue

The Holocaust was not just a Jewish tragedy although Jews above all others were marked for annihilation.[99] It was a truly human tragedy exposing the good and the bad in humanity in a way that is not usually as evident in peacetime when we are essentially independent of one another.

The Holocaust taught me that people can, through a complex series of circumstances and choices, become destructive and evil. These are the people who perpetrated the crimes against the unarmed civilians, women and children in the Holocaust. These are the people – the high-up's in Nazi leadership – who organized and ordered these crimes to be committed. These are the people who in a thousand small and large ways assisted in carrying out these crimes in countries throughout Europe.

The evil of the Holocaust was not restricted to Nazi leaders. Without the active cooperation of many people the Holocaust could not have occurred or at least could not have assumed the gigantic dimensions it did. The Gestapo for example usually had no way of knowing who was and who was not Jewish. They relied heavily on local people to point out the Jews to them and thus knowingly condemned them to their hideous fate.

People lacking in conscience helped the Nazis identify the Jews. They targeted these vulnerable members of society for robbery and even death. They also acted as the hit men for the Nazis. One of the chief architects of the Holocaust, Heinrich Himmler, preferred native volunteers called HIVIS to kill the Jews whenever possible because he was con-

---

[99] To paraphrase Elie Wiesel, "Although all Jews were victims, not all victims were Jews."

159

cerned about the effect the killing of men, women and children would have on the Germans. Many of these Hivis who were deeply destructive and virulently bigoted participated eagerly in these killings.

When the Jews of Eastern European countries were rounded up into tiny ghettos and put on starvation rations people tried to survive by scavenging for food outside the ghettoes. Older children, still small enough to be lifted up over the barriers separating the ghetto from the town were given money and valuables and sent out to exchange them for much needed food. Certain people – called '*Szmalcowniks*' in Poland – saw this situation as an opportunity to do evil. They circled around the ghetto walls like hawks in search of prey looking for these starving children. Sometimes tricking them with offers of shelter, they robbed them of their meager possessions and handed them over to the Gestapo. In some cases they simply murdered them. They also looked for Jewish faces in restaurants, train stations and on the street to rob and even kill them. In my town of Krosno, the well-to-do Herzig family and my own cousin Malka Fruhman were offered hiding places and then robbed and killed.

The Holocaust taught me many things but it did not reveal to me the source of the bottomless evil I witnessed. Reflecting on those tragic years I am even now, sixty years later, unable to comprehend how murder on such a scale and with such brutality could have occurred in the 20th Century. Psychologists and historians have tried in vain to find an explanation. How could highly educated Germans with doctorate degrees, some with double doctorates, conceive, plan, organize and participate in the implementation of such mass murder? Have German teaching institutions and universities educated their students in mass murder? How could for example a certain Dr. John Paul Kremer, a docent at the University of Muenster, as he describes in his own diary participate in the selections for the gas chambers of hundreds of babies, women and children in a few hours on an afternoon – and then that same evening attend parties and concerts?

How could he as he himself described in his own words select a number of prisoners for euthanasia by phenol injection into the heart in order to receive, "fresh specimens of liver spleen and pancreas for his research?" The eighteen victims were photographed before the injections were given to them. How could a professor of anatomy at the University of Strasbourg request perfect skull specimens from Auschwitz most certainly knowing that his request would result in the selection and killing of the appropriate prisoners?

Many thousands of highly educated men and women participated in these inhumane murders. How did these citizens arrive at such a state of disconnection from their own humanity? Were they trained in cruelty and horror by the Nazi Professors who replaced the non-Nazi teachers at all the major universities?

It is also sad to me and strange that members of the medical profession – my own profession – joined the Nazi Party in Hitler's Germany in greater numbers in terms of percentage than any other profession. When rejected for a position at the University of Muenster, Kremer complained that as, "the first Docent at the University to join the Party" he should have gotten the job with open arms. And Dr. Kremer had the audacity to refer to the allied bombings as terrorism. Can anyone explain that to me?

Thousands of volunteers from the many nationalities willingly became murderers of women and children and old people and even anxiously awaited such duties in order to get an extra ration of booze and cigarettes. How could they participate in such murder and go back to their families and children.

Why is it that of those assigned to murderous tasks in the camps, so few chose not to participate? I have wracked my brain trying to find some rational explanation for this. How could a society steeped in culture, civilized and industrialized that gave the world some of the greatest thinkers, artists and so on – many of whom were Jews – a people held in admiration by Jews metamorphose within a few years into killers? Where was their humanity? Did it just evaporate or was it not there to begin with? How could humanity, a God given gift to mankind, be so erased almost overnight? Nothing in my experience gives me answers to these questions.

Horrific as the experience of the Holocaust was, it also taught me that there are good and true human beings living at the opposite end of the spectrum from the twisted souls who perpetuated and carried out the massive destruction of those years.

These were the people who risked their lives and the lives of their families to help the victims of the Holocaust. These were the people who protected Jews by hiding them in their houses or by assisting them in hiding in the forests and by leaving food for them. They did these things for a number of reasons - some were simply appalled and disgusted by the cruelty they saw happening around them. Others acted out of Christian principles and ideals of human charity. Others acted for mixed reasons

162

including the hope of remuneration. These people saved lives, regardless of the reason. Taken together, the good and the bad people at either pole comprised only a minority, perhaps ten percent of the population. The vast majority of people were those in between. The people who did not see what was going on or who refused to hear the news. They were indifferent. Not that the evil wasn't there – right in front of their eyes and ears. They just didn't care or weren't able to notice it.

And this in itself is a kind of evil – though a lesser form perhaps than the consciously destructive evil of the perpetrators. In many if not in most instances especially in the East even if they didn't actively participate in the atrocities they were actually pleased to see the Nazis destroy the Jews who had so successfully competed in their society.

People of all nationalities and religions participated in the Holocaust. Sweden and Switzerland, supposedly neutral countries in the war, continued to have dealings with Hitler and supplied him with the materials that enabled him to wage war and commit these crimes. Even among the Western allies in France, Belgium, Holland, Denmark and Norway certain parts of the citizenry formed volunteer SS units to fight alongside Hitler's SS. In many of these countries local people participated in the rounding up of the Jews. Churches, religious institutions and individual clergy who knew what was going on also turned a blind eye and deaf ear to the tragedy. They kept silent. After the war they offered apologies. After the war it was too late.

What does all this teach us? It teaches us that we all have an obligation to notice what is going on around us and to be sensitive to the well being of others. It teaches us the need to communicate more effectively with the silent majority, the 90 percent who could have made a difference if they noticed what was happening. Even the Nazis were mindful and were constantly monitoring public opinion. Seeing no opposition to their evil deeds they had no hesitation to pursue the annihilation of the Jews.[100]

In a poem called "Pawel and Gawel," the great Polish poet Adam Mickewicz describes two inseparable friends who shared even a single nut that they foraged in the forest. When during one of their excursions a bear came upon them, Pawel, the strong one, climbed up a tree but Gawel was not strong enough to do the same.

He begged Pawel to help him up the tree but Pawel, seeing the bear approaching did not respond. Gawel in desperation threw himself on the ground feigning death – a trick he had learned in the Boy Scouts. The bear came close and started sniffing around Gawel's face, ears and taking him for dead walked away. Pawel came down from the tree. "What was the bear doing sniffing around you like that?"

"The bear whispered in my ear that you can only recognize a good friend when in need," Gawel told him. Where was humanity when we needed it?

I was visiting with Mrs. Schindler in the early 1980s and somebody asked her, "What made you do what you did during the war to help the Jews?" And she answered: *"Ganz einfach, Menschlichkeit,"* which translates, "Very simply, humanity." She added, "Isn't that expected of everybody?"

---

[100] Even a silent opposition would have helped but it wasn't there. Where was humanity in those dark years? Had it simply evaporated or was it not there to begin with? Where was the "Love thy neighbor (or friend) as you love yourself," a principle taught in every religion? What happened to "Do unto others as you would have them do unto you?"

There are numerous stories of interviews with people all over the world, people who helped so many to survive the Holocaust and each answered the question in a similar way. That is the message of this book just the same as my father's parting words to me, *"Be a mensch."*

We are told that we are born in the image of our Creator. If this is true then we are endowed with His attributes of Goodness, Charity and Love. These attributes are included so to say in our genetic code. But we must nurture and develop these attributes in ourselves and in our children.

Had the German people and the peace-loving world listened carefully and responded more quickly to the rhetoric of hate preached by the Nazis in the early 1920s history might have been different. That rhetoric might not have become a full-scale program of action as it did beginning in 1933. The importance of paying attention to such a political movement however small cannot be overemphasized. Bosnia and Iraq are contemporary examples. To avoid the chance of such a movement beginning again even in a democracy like the United States we must fulfill our obligations of citizenship including the right and obligation to vote. We must select and vote for the candidate who will best represent and guard the important principles embodied in our Constitution and our Bill of Rights.

Like so many other Holocaust "survivors," I lost my entire family. Nevertheless, from the perspective of my odyssey through those tragic years my experiences must be regarded as less horrific than those of many other survivors – due partly to my imprisonment at the German Luftwaffe over the entire year of 1943 and my transfer to Schindler's camp where I lived from October of 1944 to May of 1945. In both of these places the conditions were relatively humane and miraculously killings did not occur.

My own more "benign" view of the different nationalities stems also from the fact that I worked with some good Germans and other nationals. I am less inclined to hold an entire people responsible than are those unfortunate victims who were continually exposed to the gruesome work of the SS murderers and their assistants. Very simply I am unable to harbor hate. My father was the same.

Forgetting is another matter. How can I forget even now sixty years later? How can I forget the face of my eleven-year-old brother with tears flowing as he was being led away from us? How can I forget how my father turned around to see us for the last time before being led away to the gas chambers of Auschwitz?

How can I forget coming home one evening from forced labor duties and finding my mother and sister gone forever, shot at a nearby mass grave? How does one forget the shooting of the young mother Rachel with both her babies in her arms only yards away from where her husband and I were standing in December of 1942? Am I also to forget the others lying around bleeding into the dirt and the snow, shot at point blank range? How is one to continue living, raising a family and enjoying one's friends, family and grandchildren, after such an experience?

It all comes back to me even now especially in the silence of sleepless nights, when my guard is down and I am vulnerable to the tormenting images of those years. I might forgive but I can never forget. No amount of apologies or restitution can make me forget those horrible experiences or those inhumanities. I can only take them with me to the grave.

We have the obligation to fight against such atrocities in the future. Our humanity, endowed to us by our Creator must be nourished and nurtured in all our children at home, in schools, churches, temples, mosques and other institutions. We must not allow our humanity to be deformed as it was in the camps. We must continually remind ourselves of our humanity so that we do not fall prey to radical ideas of Nazism, Communism and other potentially dehumanizing ideologies.

Has humanity learned the lesson? Obviously not judging from what goes on in the world today. Should we give up? Absolutely not! We should redouble our efforts to stem the terrorism and killing. Hopefully our children will see the results of our efforts.

Amen.

Inez – my future wife
in 1943 at age 10 (above)
and in 1950 at
HS graduation (below)

1953 at Fort Sam Houston, Texas. In the left picture I am sitting in a friend's car.

Texas Gulf Coast

With Dr. Jablonski from Poland, a Holocaust survivor I knew in Munich and who I happened to meet at Fort Sam Houston.

Denise, Les, Alex, Julie and Inez White - 1964

Denise, Les, Julie, Inez and Alex White - 1968

Alex and Inez – 1958
on Italy vacation

Speaking at a
Convention in Chicago

Son, Les (above) and
a smiling and elegant Inez (right)

Cousin Mark Fruhman from Krosno.
He lived in Manchester, England and he
fought with the Anders Polish Army in
North Africa and Monte Cassino

Speaking at a
Holocaust Memorial
Service in Chicago

Chicago – with Medical Practice Colleagues

Daughter Julie – Naval Officer
and Gulf War Veteran

Daughter Denise who works
in Scottsdale, Arizona

Alex and Inez White

Dr. Alexander Bialywlos White

L to R: Les (*son*), Inez, Julie (*daughter*),
Jay North (*Julie's husband*) and Alex White.

At home in Scottsdale, Arizona

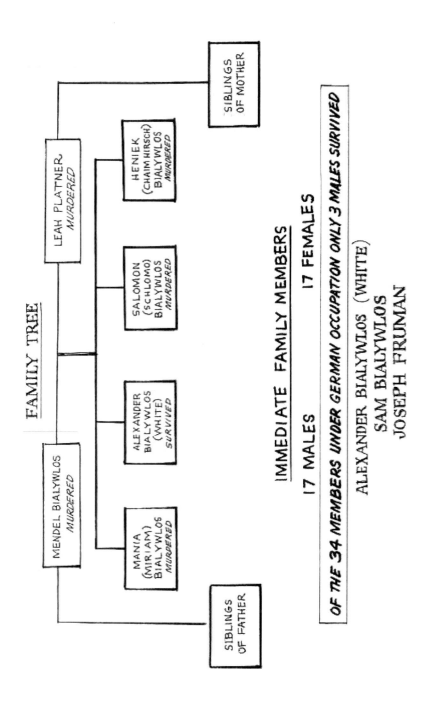

FAMILY TREE

MENDEL BIALYWLOS
MURDERED

LEAH PLATNER
MURDERED

SIBLINGS OF MOTHER

SIBLINGS OF FATHER

MANIA (MIRIAM) BIALYWLOS
MURDERED

ALEXANDER BIALYWLOS (WHITE)
SURVIVED

SALOMON (SCHLOMO) BIALYWLOS
MURDERED

HENIEK (CHAIM HIRSCH) BIALYWLOS
MURDERED

IMMEDIATE FAMILY MEMBERS

17 MALES   17 FEMALES

OF THE 34 MEMBERS UNDER GERMAN OCCUPATION ONLY 3 MALES SURVIVED

ALEXANDER BIALYWLOS (WHITE)
SAM BIALYWLOS
JOSEPH FRUMAN